EXPLORING CAREERS IN COMPUTER SOFTWARE

By

Dorothy Brockman

THE ROSEN PUBLISHING GROUP, INC.

NEW YORK

Published in 1985 by The Rosen Publishing Group
29 East 21st Street, New York City, New York 10010

First Edition   *52136*
Copyright 1985 by Dorothy Brockman

Library of Congress Cataloging in Publication Data

Brockman, Dorothy.
    Exploring careers in computer software.

    1. Computer software industry—Vocational guidance.
I. Title.
HD9696.C62B76   1985   001.64′25′02373   85-8258
ISBN 0-8239-0653-1

Manufactured in the United States of America

Cover photo courtesy of Wanda Fielder

88 - 16704

Contents

	Introduction	v
I.	*Helpful Aptitudes and Attitudes*	1
II.	*The Software Marketers*	13
III.	*The Software Entrepreneur*	17
IV.	*Who Are the Software Creators?*	25
V.	*High School—A Time to Seek Out the Target*	48
VI.	*Higher Education—A Chance of a Lifetime*	99
VII.	*Artificial Intelligence: Building the Software of the Future?*	117
VIII.	*Potential Employers*	129
	Glossary	153

The author wishes to dedicate this book to the founder of Universal Computer Systems—a man whose tireless enthusiasm for his work, technical brilliance, and keen organizational skills have led to his successful career as a builder and marketer of computer software.

Introduction

If you are wondering whether a career in computer software is for you, this book will help you make that decision. Whether or not you ultimately decide to be an "insider" within the software industry, computers will have a considerable impact on your life. As the cost of the physical hardware continues to plummet, the market for the software that drives the circuitry is skyrocketing. In the years ahead, software designers, writers, and marketers will be in great demand to produce and sell computer programs for the desk-top microprocessors that have flooded the market. Thousands of programmers are already at work creating "user-friendly" software packages that integrate into one system such wonderful capabilities as word processing, three-dimensional graphics, spreadsheets, databases, and electronic mail.

Leaders from academia and the computer industry have a remarkable vision of your future in the "electronic universe." They speak of factories that are controlled by computers and of great worldwide networks of communicating home and business computers. They predict the continued development of many more expert computer systems primed with the knowledge of the highly educated. And they even prophesy the coming of "intelligent" computers that will possess learning and reasoning abilities.

To fulfill dreams such as these, outstanding applications and systems programmers, systems analysts, software engineers, database and data communications experts, knowledge engineers, and researchers of all kinds will have to be trained from your generation—the graduates of the 1980s and beyond. Whether you see yourself as a systems analyst designing business software, as a software development engineer creating programs that help to manage the factory of the future, as a regional sales manager leading a high-tech marketing force, or as a knowledge engineer building expert systems, you will need sophisticated skills to achieve your goals.

Since you will have to invest a great deal of time and effort to become a software specialist, you must take a realistic look at your capabilities and interests to determine whether you wish to spend the rest of your working life in this industry. To help you decide if you "fit the profile," the first chapter of this book discusses some of the aptitudes and attitudes of many of the people currently in software creation and sales.

Chapter II examines the all-important marketers who get the software products to the public, followed by a chapter on the entrepreneurs who dare to form new companies. To enhance your understanding of what software professionals do, Chapter IV describes the major job categories within the industry. By reading this (slightly) technical section, you should add to your vocabulary of computerese (computer jargon).

Chapter V discusses how to target yourself toward a software career as early as high school. Next, Chapter VI examines computer-oriented college majors, names several of the academic leaders in the field, and discusses some aspects of the two-year associate degree. In an effort to glimpse the future, Chapter VII highlights some of the accomplishments of the artificial intelligence community, and the last chapter looks at the types of companies that employ software talent.

About the Author

Dorothy Brockman, a graduate of the University of Minnesota, is a Vice President and Director of Universal Computer Systems, Inc. As a COBOL programmer, she assisted in the founding of UCS in 1970. Mrs. Brockman also is a registered principal with a member firm of the National Association of Securities Dealers, Inc., and was formerly a registered associate representative with a New York Stock Exchange firm.

Universal Computer Systems, Inc. offers batch and on-line computer services and mainframe in-house computer systems to customers throughout the U.S. The company is a recognized leader in the development of automotive data processing. An industry innovator, UCS built the first "instant update" on-line parts inventory and accounting system for car dealers.

Using terminals linked to high-speed dedicated phone lines, UCS customers are connected to a huge distributed database of automobile parts inventories, a portion of which is located at the company's central site in Houston and part of which is on computer disks at individual car dealerships across the country.

As a computer systems integrator for the automotive industry, UCS specializes in buying IBM mainframe central processors, terminals, printers, and other equipment and bundling these components together with extremely sophisticated systems and proprietary applications software to create a complete computer system with data communications capabilities.

Chapter 1

Helpful Aptitudes and Attitudes

There are those among you who are capable of making outstanding contributions to a dream—a vision of universal information conveyed at speeds approaching the speed of light where every inquiring mind has instant access via a computer to the knowledge of all the libraries of the world.

For the developed countries, this goal from out of science fiction's past is becoming a reality. With one amazing breakthrough after another, technology is pushing us toward nationwide, even worldwide, data communications (DC). One such step toward international teleprocessing is the development of the IBM-sponsored European Academic Research Network. This network, according to IBM, will link university scientists and IBM research facilities in Europe and the U.S.

Another interesting contribution toward the dream of instant, "on-tap" information is the huge effort presently under way to put all seventeen volumes of the *Oxford English Dictionary* on a computer *database* (electronic file). Privileged computer owners with special communications *hardware* (equipment) and *software* (programs) will be able to access this wonderful resource over telephone lines.

Such networks of computing machines, which are able to retrieve information from databases like the *Oxford English Dictionary*, even now are spreading over the globe. It is the job of a chosen few, the software builders, to bring these complex systems to life.

Some of you will be tomorrow's talented software designers and writers; you will program powerful problem-solving solutions into computers. Your *programs* (the instructions that detail computer actions) will enable these machines to work for us in vital new ways. Without such "life-giving" software, even a multimillion-dollar Cray supercomputer would be totally useless.

What you want to consider here is whether your aptitudes and attitudes are suited to the development of these computer programs. Before you invest your money and priceless time in extensive training to become a software creator, you must determine whether you would enjoy a lifetime of working with electronic machines.

If you enter this profession, you will want to make a positive contribution. A mediocre *systems analyst* (software designer) or *programmer* (the person who actually writes the computer instructions) can be a threat to himself, his employer, and society. By overlooking the tiniest detail, he can loop a figurative noose around his neck. That is because computers magnify errors. If a programmer puts the wrong mathematical formula into a computer, *every time* the machine uses that formula it will produce a wrong answer. Even a personal computer, not to mention a powerful mainframe, can spit out thousands, even millions, of egregious errors in a very short time. And who gets the blame? You can bet that it will not be the "poor" ignorant machine.

So try to take an honest look at yourself as you attempt to determine if you have the "programmer/systems analyst's aptitude." Later, I will examine the work of both systems analysts and programmers to help you decide whether you would enjoy one of these jobs.

Some of you may elect instead to go into software sales. The future entrepreneurs among you may dream of combining design, programming, and marketing skills to start your own business. I will discuss these last two exciting options later.

To help you understand what *aptitudes* are important for success as a software builder, I asked a *data processing* (DP) manager with eighteen years' experience what talents he believed are vital to a systems analyst or a programmer. Here are his comments:

"Logical ability is a great asset to a programmer, and so is a good memory. A fine programmer can find efficient solutions to complex problems. She is able to skillfully handle several mental tasks simultaneously.

"Some programming aptitude tests attempt to measure logical ability through the use of sequence and pattern questions. Although there is disagreement over the use of these tests, anyone who is considering programming as a profession should ask herself whether she enjoys this type of mental puzzle.

"A few companies discount or refuse entirely to give such tests; one software house claims that one of its brightest and most productive employees failed such a data processing aptitude test. Many organizations, however, do put great faith in aptitude tests if they are properly and fairly administered.

"I have noticed that my score improves each time I take one of these tests. Although I would like to believe otherwise, I doubt that I am getting smarter."

"Can high motivation compensate for weakness in these areas?" I ask.

"The desire to do well in any field is one of the most important factors for success, but you asked me to name aptitudes. Some programmers can complete a project in three weeks; others with similar work experience have to spend much longer. If all other factors are equal, which one would you want working for you?"

Are all factors *ever* equal? I think to myself. Then I say: "Although I am skeptical of generalizations, I suppose that a programmer with a good memory and a knack for seeing cause-and-effect relationships should be able to create better code quicker than someone who lacks superior logic and/or memory skills."

One company that has designed a series of data processing tests that are used by many organizations is Psychometrics, Inc., of Santa Monica, California. Data processing employers use the Berger Aptitude for Programming Test (B-APT), the Berger Tests of Programming Proficiency (B-TOPP), and the Berger Systems Analyst General Evaluation (B-SAGE) tests to help make vital personnel decisions.

According to the company's co-directors, psychologists Frances R. and Raymond M. Berger, "the Berger Aptitude for Programming Test is a highly valid, job-related programming aptitude test. It is designed so that even examinees with no programming background can understand the test's programming language required to solve the problems.

"The B-APT is a thirty-item job sample test requiring the examinee to learn a simple programming language and respond to problems by writing small routines according to the rules of the language. By the time the examinee gets to Part III of the B-APT, he will have been taught to code, loop, increment, and branch. The administration time for B-APT includes approximately forty-five minutes of tutorial and practice, and forty minutes of actual test-taking time."

The Bergers list many prominent organizations as users of their personnel tests. Among them are: AT&T Information Systems, American Express, Metropolitan Life, Digital Equipment Corporation, and the Departments of the Air Force, Army, and Navy. (The Bergers also do specialized test construction for the military in technical areas, not DP exclusively.) If you choose a software-oriented career, you might be given one of these data processing tests.

Many employers also administer an aptitude test designed by

Answer sheet

Computer Programmer Aptitude Battery (CPAB)

Author Jean Maier Palormo, Science Research Associates, Inc.

Sample Item
Diagramming

Sample Problem and Conditions

A. A company inspects and classifies its products in lots of 100.

B. It is necessary to classify the individual pieces within each lot of 100 into three classes by weight:

Class K — 4.5 oz. or over

Class L — 3.5 to 4.4 oz.

Class M — less than 3.5 oz.

Instructions In this section there are a number of problems with flow charts (schematic diagrams) that illustrate the process by which each problem is solved. The solution to a problem is illustrated in its diagram by following the arrows from cell to cell. Read the *Sample Problem and Conditions* above and look at the sample diagram.

Cell 1
A   Is it less than 3.5 oz ?
B   Select a piece.
C   Is it 3.5 to 4.4 oz ?
D   Classify as M
E   Classify as L

Cell 2
A   Classify as K
B   Classification of lot complete
C   Select a piece
D   Classify as M
E   Classify as L

Cell 3
A   Select a piece
B   Classification of lot complete
C   Classify lot as K
D   Classify lot as L
E   Classify lot as M

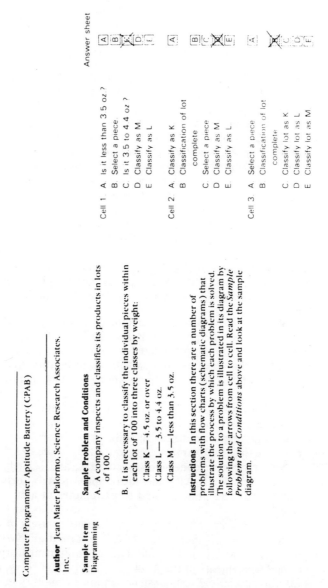

Fig. 1/1. *Section from the Computer Programmer Aptitude Battery.*

Science Research Associates, Inc., a subsidiary of IBM, called the Computer Programmer Aptitude Battery (CPAB). According to SRA, "the five subtests of CPAB measure abilities related to success in computer programmer and systems analysis fields."

The following are listed as "job-tasks tested" by CPAB: (They are reprinted courtesy of SRA from the *SRA Test Catalog for Business*, Copyright Science Research Associates, Inc. 1981. Revised 1983. By permission of the publisher.)

Verbal Meaning—knowledge of vocabulary commonly used in math, business, and systems engineering literature.

Reasoning—ability to translate ideas and operations from word problems into mathematical notations.

SCIENCE RESEARCH ASSOCIATES, INC.
A Subsidiary of IBM

Computer Programmer Aptitude Battery (CPAB)

Sample Diagram

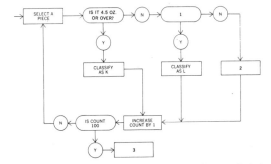

Note that some cells in the diagram contain a statement of action (e.g., "Select a piece"); some cells contain a question (e.g., "Is it 4.5 oz. or over?"); and some cells contain an answer to the question ("Y" for yes, or "N" for no). If it were complete, every cell in the diagram would contain a statement, question, or answer.

However, the diagrams as given are not complete; some cells contain a number instead of a question or statement. Your task is to complete the diagram by filling in the numbered cells so that the diagram *correctly* charts the problem solution. For each numbered cell you are given five alternative questions or statements to the right of the diagram and problem. From these alternatives you are to choose the one that should properly appear in the cell of that number.

Now look at the diagram again. The first step in solving the problem of classifying the products is to "Select a piece." Following the arrow to the next cell, the question is asked, "Is it 4.5 oz. or over?" The arrow going down from this cell leads to the answer "Y" (or yes), and then to the cell classifying the piece as K (because Class K weighs 4.5 oz. or over). Now go back to the question and follow the arrow leading to the answer "N" (or no).

This leads to the numbered cell 1, for which you must select the proper statement or question. Before looking at the suggested alternatives for this cell, look at the arrows going from it. One arrow down leads to the answer "Y" (yes) and then to a cell classifying the piece as L. These entries indicate that cell 1 must ask a question—a question that will identify the piece as Class L. The question "Is it 3.5 to 4.4 oz.?" would do this because that is the weight given for Class L. Now look at the

alternatives for cell 1. This question is listed as alternative C and the C-box on the sample answer sheet has been marked. Now look at cell 2. The arrow leading to it comes from the answer "N" (no) to the question you have just inserted in cell 1 ("Is it 3.5 to 4.4 oz.?"). In order to get to this point on the diagram the piece must have taken the following route —

Question: "Is it 4.5 oz. or over?" (A test for Class K)
Answer: No
Question: "Is it 3.5 to 4.4 oz.?" (A test for Class L)
Answer: No

Therefore, following this path in the diagram, the piece being tested is neither Class K nor Class L. It must be Class M. Now look at the alternatives for cell 2. The D-alternative, "Classify as M," is correct for cell 2 and the D-box has been marked on the sample answer sheet. Now select the proper statement or question for cell 3 yourself. *Make no marks in this test booklet.*

You should have chosen alternative B — "Classification of lot complete." According to the problem, all 100 pieces in a lot need to be inspected and classified. Notice in the diagram that each time you classify a piece, either K, L, or M, the arrow leads you to the cell containing the statement "Increase count by 1," and then to the cell "Is count 100?" If the answer to this question is "N," the arrow goes to the beginning of the diagram and another piece is selected for inspection and classification. However, when this process has been repeated 100 times, the count is increased to 100, and the answer to the question is "Y." Then all pieces in the lot have been classified and the lot is complete.

COURTESY SCIENCE RESEARCH ASSOCIATES, INC.

Fig. 1/2. *Section from the Computer Programmer Aptitude Battery.*

Letter Series—ability to reason abstractly, to find a pattern in a given series of letters.

Number Ability—ability to quickly estimate reasonable answers to computations.

Diagramming—ability to analyze a problem and order the steps for solution in a logical sequence.

Although SRA does not sell tests to private individuals, the company gave me permission to reproduce the sample diagramming problem in Figures 1/1–1/2.

One of our most brilliant systems programmers good-naturedly subjected himself to a programming aptitude test from another company, Tridata Corporation, 3057 College Heights Boulevard, Allentown, PA 18104. The intent was to test the test, *not* the programmer. Although we used the written version, it is also available for the IBM Personal Computer (PC). Predictably, his score was perfect.

Tridata gave permission to reproduce a sample programming aptitude test question; see Figure 1/3. The company says that Problem 4 is of medium difficulty (the answer to the problem is 20).

Ask your high school counselor for professional advice in this area. She should have your scores on tests that indicate verbal, logical, and mathematical aptitude. An understanding of English and a strong math aptitude are a definite advantage.

Although you may not need calculus to be an excellent commercial programmer, you do need a solid business math background. At present, there are plenty of programmers in the field who will admit in private to math anxiety. In the future, however, you will have to compete for the best jobs with applicants who have overcome that problem.

If you wish to major in computer science at a four-year college, you had best have higher math under your belt. Since scientific programmers and designers are required to have a degree in computer science, information science, engineering, math, or one of the physical sciences, they need an excellent score on the math section of the SAT to complete one of these demanding college programs. The above majors are discussed in detail in the chapter on higher education.

In both the scientific and business communities, programmers are required to handle program definitions of great length and complexity. For this reason, a good memory is a valuable asset; sometimes it can compensate for weaknesses in other areas. One programmer who is noted for his ability to recall detail bragged to me that although he did not understand or remember one equation from his college calculus course, he had made an A. When I skeptically inquired how he had managed this remarkable feat, he said he had memorized the formulas and applied the appropriate equation to the correct problem.

"I hope you don't use that technique in your programming!" I quipped.

"Of course not!" he laughed. "My programs make sense; I have a logical reason for every action that I tell the computer to take."

High clerical aptitude is another capability that employers look

TEST OVERVIEW

The Tridata Programmer Aptitude Test is an exercise in logic and the ability to follow instructions. PASE will help to indicate your programming potential without the need to know a computer programming language.

This test presents eight exercises that test your ability to think logically. The thought process you go through to solve these exercises is similar to the process you would use to develop sections of computer programs. Therefore, your ability to solve these exercises would be a good indicator of your ability to understand or even to write complex computer programs.

To make these exercises less abstract, they are presented in the form of an allegory. The next paragraph contains the basic premise of this allegory.

As an employee of the PASE Moving Company you are instructed to move the residents of a row of ten townhouses. The townhouses have sequential addresses ranging from 1 to 10. The number of residents living in the townhouses are indicated by the number in the house. For each row of townhouses you are given a set of directions that instruct you to perform arithmetic operations on the numbers residing in the houses. You must follow the directions exactly to finish with the correct number in the designated townhouse. You should follow the directions downward unless instructed otherwise.

Turn page and review sample problem before starting test. Good luck!

Fig. 1/3.   *Four pages from the Programmer Aptitude Self Evaluation.*

for in a programming applicant. This skill is important because programmer analysts must pay very close attention to detail. A *bug* (a defect caused by an omission or error) in the program can lie like an explosive mine waiting for the right test-condition (set of circumstances) to set it off.

Software creators also need high powers of concentration and excellent organizational abilities in order to hold in their mind a

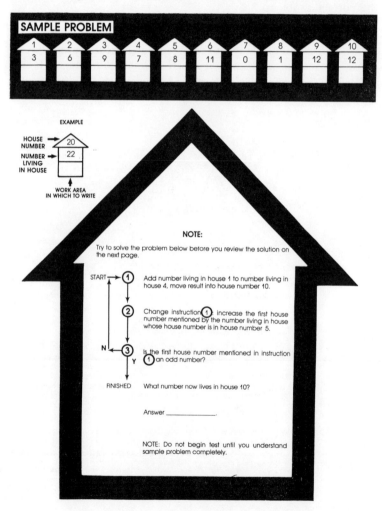

SAMPLE PROBLEM

1	2	3	4	5	6	7	8	9	10
3	6	9	7	8	11	0	1	12	12

EXAMPLE

HOUSE NUMBER → 20
NUMBER LIVING IN HOUSE → 22

WORK AREA IN WHICH TO WRITE

NOTE:

Try to solve the problem below before you review the solution on the next page.

START → ① Add number living in house 1 to number living in house 4, move result into house number 10.

② Change instruction ①: increase the first house number mentioned by the number living in house whose house number is in house number 5.

N ← ③ Is the first house number mentioned in instruction ① an odd number?
Y

FINISHED What number now lives in house 10?

Answer _____.

NOTE: Do not begin test until you understand sample problem completely.

number of alternatives that the computer might take depending on some predetermined condition. For example, consider the following COBOL statement, which I excerpted from a "live" inventory control program:

IF H-ORDER-THIS-CYCLE-YES

   IF P-PART-COST > 5.00

      IF P-BIN-LOCATION-UPSTAIRS

         IF P-WEEKS-SINCE-LAST-SALE < 2

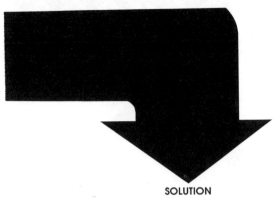

SOLUTION

A. Instruction No. ①: The number in house 1 is 3. The number living in house 4 is 7. (3 + 7 = 10); move the result (10) into house 10. The number 12 is now replaced by the number 10 in house number 10.

B. Instruction No. ②: Requests that you change Instruction No. ① directions. The first house number mentioned in Instruction No. ① is house 1. You are asked to increase this number. The number residing in house number 5 (which is 8) directs you to house number 8 where the proper number to increment house 1 resides (1). Therefore, we increase house 1 in Instruction No. ① by 1. Instruction No. ① should read:

> "Add number living in house 2 to number living in house 4, move result into house number 10."

C. Instruction No. ③: The first house number mentioned in Instruction No. ① is now 2, so the answer to the question is NO. The arrow pointing to "N" (for a "no" answer) directs you back to Instruction No. ①.

D. Instruction No. ①: The number living in house 2 is 6. The number living in house 4 is 7. (6 + 7 = 13); move result (13) into house number 10. The number 10 is now replaced by number 13 in house number 10.

E. Instruction No. ②: Once again, you are asked to change the directions in Instruction No. ①. As directed in explanation B (above). You will increase the first house mentioned in Instruction No. ① (which is now house 2) by the number living in house 8 (which is still 1). Instruction No. ① will now read:

> "Add number living in house 3 to number living in house 4, move result into house number 10."

F. Instruction No. ③: The first house number in Instruction No. ① is now an odd number. Go to finish. The number living in house 10 is 13. ANSWER = 13.

IF P-ANNUAL-RATE-OF-SALE > 22
PERFORM ORDER-CALCULATION

THRU PLACE-ORDER-IF-ANY

ELSE GO TO BYPASS-ALL-ORDERS.

This COBOL code is more straightforward than it appears at first glance. If *all* of the "IF" conditions are true, the computer will

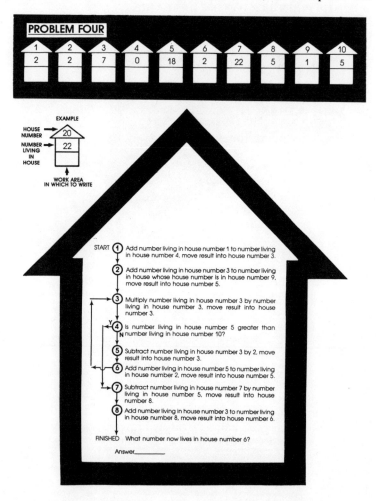

PROBLEM FOUR

1	2	3	4	5	6	7	8	9	10
2	2	7	0	18	2	22	5	1	5

EXAMPLE

HOUSE NUMBER → 20
NUMBER LIVING IN HOUSE → 22

↓

WORK AREA IN WHICH TO WRITE

START (1) Add number living in house number 1 to number living in house number 4, move result into house number 3.

(2) Add number living in house number 3 to number living in house whose house number is in house number 9, move result into house number 5.

(3) Multiply number living in house number 3 by number living in house number 3, move result into house number 3.

Y (4) Is number living in house number 5 greater than N number living in house number 10?

(5) Subtract number living in house number 3 by 2, move result into house number 3.

(6) Add number living in house number 5 to number living in house number 2, move result into house number 5.

(7) Subtract number living in house number 7 by number living in house number 5, move result into house number 8.

(8) Add number living in house number 3 to number living in house number 8, move result into house number 6.

FINISHED What number now lives in house number 6?

Answer_____

execute the instructions from "ORDER-CALCULATION" through the last instruction under "PLACE-ORDER-IF-ANY." If *any* one of the "IF" conditions is false, the machine executes "BYPASS-ALL-ORDERS," bypassing all of the "PERFORM" statements included in "ORDER-CALCULATION" through PLACE-ORDER -IF-ANY."

If you feel that you have the above aptitudes, working with computers may give you a challenging opportunity to excel. Your ability to quickly grasp a myriad factors and organize them in a logical order could lead you to an interesting and creative life's work. And there is a big bonus: You will be well paid.

You may have the capabilities to be a programmer/systems analyst yet to be otherwise unsuited to the rigors of working with computers. To be frank, some people love this type of work and others despise it. The people who do enjoy it say that they delight in using their mental skills to *create*. They take pleasure in solving difficult problems for others, and most important, they have great pride of workmanship. In fact, this desire for creative excellence may be the single most important factor that motivates people in this field.

One commercial systems analyst told me that he liked the feeling of power he experienced when he was designing a computer system to create order out of chaos. This ability to write the software that makes the computer "think" can be a potent ego builder. Once you have taught a computer to solve a business problem, the machine will pump out answers and reports faster than a whole army of bookkeepers and typists.

Think of the creative power of a scientist programming a computer to solve a difficult problem. This partnership of a skilled human and a complex machine can inspire awe in almost anyone: Imagine, for example, the thrill of contributing to the design of one of the computer systems that guide our nation's space shuttles.

The Bergers have devised "special DP [data processing] questionnaires that cover and pinpoint *interests* in specific DP areas. Called the Berger Questionnaire (B-QUEST), it is an interests inventory assessing the match between a person's work-related interests and various DP jobs.

"The Form G assumes no prior experience in data processing. The inventory asks the individual to indicate a level of interest or liking for various DP and non-DP job activities. Form S is designed for those who have some previous experience in data processing. It focuses in depth on specific DP activities, including applications and systems programming, operations, systems analysis, sales and management." Ask your school guidance counselor or corporate human resource official about this newly developed questionnaire.

Since exponential change is typical in the computer industry, a software professional needs to crave new knowledge. Ideally, he should enjoy the intellectual challenge of attempting to keep abreast of the continual, rapid technological breakthroughs. In fact, to advance or even hold his ground a systems analyst and even a programmer must keep informed about the new types of computer software and hardware available. That is no easy task!

A software creator who achieves a high degree of expertise usually will admit that he enjoys being an authority in his field. As such, he sometimes has the exciting opportunity "to be there" at the leading edge of technology as it advances.

For such rewards there is a price to pay: It is called commitment to task. A good software builder can become so involved in the mental puzzle of instructing a computer that she detaches herself from the rest of the world and works alone for hours, even days at a time—usually under pressure. While her friends bask in the sun, she works indoors, often in a small space, using her mind to broaden her horizons. Dedication alone is not enough. Her code must be extremely precise. At times, she is on the job at night or on weekends to finish, test, and de-bug her work. She is task-oriented.

Some software creators would rather program than do almost anything else you can name. I know a programmer—he is one of the best and most respected I have ever met—who writes code 349 days a year. He often works around the clock without sleep. On Christmas day, when the rest of us are opening our presents, he is at the computer center.

And what do you think he has in his office at home? An IBM PC/XT (a personal computer with the added memory capacity of a hard, as opposed to floppy, disk). Do you think this man loves his work? We think so.

Although he is exceptional, there are more people like him in the computer industry than you might think. He began his career by making top grades in his college computer courses. With no plans to get a degree, he went to work as a programmer. Fearlessly, he tackled the most complicated *systems software* (the programs that supervise the inner workings of the machine). He had to know exactly what made the computer tick. Within five years he was promoted to Vice President of Programming, with a salary to match his title. Although few college graduates could compete with this brilliant, self-taught systems programmer, the majority of us need that diploma.

Chapter II

The Software Marketers

Do you have aspirations to be the President of International Business Machines Corporation? If so—great! BUT, you had better be one super salesman! You cannot be president of the world's most powerful computer company unless you have worked your way up the sales ladder. Even IBM needs customers.

Exactly what do software marketers do? They sell solutions to problems. If a salesman is successful, he can make a great deal of money. As king of the hill, his persuasive powers are in great demand. If, however, he is unable to find customers for his company, he soon will be out of a job.

Ask any marketing manager, and he will tell you that "a good (sales)man is hard to find!" With the rewards of success so great, why is this so? The answer is that it takes a special kind of determined person to turn a skeptical prospect into a smiling customer.

A number of years ago, I first had the privilege of observing such a resolute salesman in action. As a child, his family was so destitute that he was forced to face his jeering schoolmates with no shoes. By the time he reached high school, he had a burning desire to go to college to pull himself out of poverty. He lacked even the money for a bus ticket, but he had one hope: He loomed tall on the football field. So, when the coach said: "If you want an athletic-work scholarship, go kill the quarterback," the huge left end struck terror in the hearts of the opposing team's backfield.

Four years later, with his college degree in hand, he landed his first job as a mutual fund salesman. Stocks are like software in one obvious way: They are an intangible product. As his first prospect the new salesman picked the dignified town undertaker. Having been burned in the stock market in his youth, the gray-haired undertaker was determined never to buy stock again, period.

Do you think that this wealthy businessman was an impossible prospect? The determined salesman saw him as a worthy challenge.

One year and twenty-three sales calls later, the undertaker whipped out his checkbook and bought $250,000 worth of mutual funds. How did this pleasant but tenacious salesman win over his reluctant prospect? By "simply" convincing him that he needed the product! During each visit, the salesman presented one or two advantages of the mutual fund form of stock ownership—and quickly left. Eventually, he had the prospect asking questions—the right questions. At the end of a year, the strong, friendly salesman had "educated" his prospect.

Like the stock salesman, the software marketing representative must provide his busy, skeptical prospect with concise yet comprehensive answers. As a salesman of sophisticated, high-tech computer systems, his job is dependent on his understanding of his product. An unprepared software salesman who thinks that he can get by on his gift of gab is in for a humbling experience. Computer software often is expensive and extremely complicated. Perceptive buyers of commercial and scientific systems have an uncanny ability to ask pointed questions that cuttingly reveal a salesman's lack of product knowledge.

I asked an extremely successful sales manager of a Houston software company what personality traits and abilities he hopes to find when he interviews an applicant for a job selling computer services. Here is his reply:

"I look for a salesman or woman who makes a good first impression. I am a believer in the traditional IBM businessman's dress code for salesmen: tie, white cotton shirt, wool or lightweight wool suit, and even a vest for men gives a professional appearance. A saleswoman also should present a conservative, well-tailored appearance that instills confidence.

"The ideal candidate has a dynamic personality. Friendly and outgoing, he enjoys working with people. He is positive, confident, and able to command attention. Sensitive to the reactions of others, he is an excellent communicator who can explain his complex software solutions with elegant simplicity. This is not an easy task. If he is to earn his prospect's trust, his manner must be disarming, and his facts have to be intellectually persuasive. Self-assured, he has learned to face his fears. Putting them behind him, he is persistent without being overly aggressive. He will call on a well-qualified prospect as many times as necessary to sell him. Why? Because he has a burning desire to achieve. And he wants to be rich—very rich.

"I hope to find a sales applicant who is very well organized. The more organized a salesman is, the more sales calls he is able to make in one day. If he keeps detailed records on each sales call, he will improve his 'memory' of each prospect's name, his particular problems, and his comments.

"A software salesman must be a teacher. As a technical salesman, he must be able to explain the complicated concepts and intricacies of how his software will fulfill the prospect's needs. The potential customer will not buy the software until he has been 'educated' as to how the product will benefit him.

"For this reason, a software salesperson must have an in-depth technical knowledge, not only of the software service or product that he is selling, but also of his prospect's type of business. That requires homework. If, for example, he is selling a payroll applications package, he had better know his tax calculations. If his product is inventory control, he must be able to explain how his software's stock replenishment formula will work for his prospect's specialized inventory.

"A salesman who can foresee and answer a potential customer's questions and objections is headed in the right direction. Some prospects can do a great job of listing reasons why they should buy another product. For this reason, a salesman had better be aware of his competitors' strengths and weaknesses. He must be able to show that, for the price, his software is the best buy. He may try to prove his point by showing that his product has superior, easy-to-use features and excellent *documentation* (explanatory information). If he is trying to sell a very complicated computer system, he had better be able to provide a long list of references willing to praise, not only his programs, but his installation and service departments as well.

"Let me make one last comment. If you go to work for a company that offers superior software products, your life will be a lot easier than if you attempt to sell mediocre packages or services. I like to think that I am doing my customers a favor."

Many software salesmen say that they thoroughly enjoy their work. If they are successful they have the opportunity to make more money than most technical workers. Since salesmen usually work on a commission plan, they see a direct relationship between their efforts and their pay.

Some salespeople delight in their freedom to get out of the office or even out of town where they can meet new people. If their job involves extensive long-distance travel, this advantage can turn sour, especially if they are married. Many families find that they are unable to tolerate one member's absence over the long haul.

Unless you like earthshaking surprises, you must find out a company's relocation policies *before* you go to work as a software marketing representative. Otherwise, after a few years of dedicated service, you might be "promoted" to Timbuktu (or worse) to establish a new sales territory.

Many top management positions of the world's most successful software companies are staffed by former salesmen with a business background, an in-depth product knowledge, and a flair for dealing with people. Even the president of IBM had to start somewhere—as a salesman.

Chapter III

The Software Entrepreneur

Do you want to be the boss? It is the American dream. All you have to do is start your own business—perhaps a software company. If you are successful, you will answer to "higher authorities"—your customers—each capable of hiring and firing you at their slightest whim.

WANTED! Programmer/analysts to invent user-friendly software for the millions of families who will buy a desk-top personal computer this decade. Can you think of a brilliant new way to use one of these powerful *microprocessors*? If your idea will save time or transfer an unpleasant task to a machine, it could be the foundation for your business. In fact, a truly original idea turned into computer programs could make you wealthy. There are markets waiting to be tapped in the areas of entertainment, self-improvement, education, business, and science.

Already, other innovators have thought of hundreds of uses for *microcomputers*. Computers can regulate your home's thermostat, catch the burglar as he creeps in through your window, and turn on your oven remotely. Unquestionably, some of you will think of more exciting ideas than those.

A few of my favorite software inventions are a flight simulator that helps you learn to fly, a speed-reading course to upgrade your reading level, and a word processor that lets you correct your writing errors on the screen *before* you print the text. *The Independent Guide to IBM Personal Computers*, a magazine published by Ziff-Davis Publishing Co., One Park Avenue, New York, NY 10016, discusses many of the programs that are currently available for microprocessors. These are just the tip of the software iceberg. IBM, for example, publishes *Software Directory*, which lists more than two thousand programs for the entire range of its hardware from personal computers to mainframes.

Once you have designed and coded your new idea into a program, your work is still not finished. Your marvelous software invention must be sold. How can you get it to the public? You must face the entrepreneur's number one concern—finding customers.

If you do not wish to market your product yourself, you must find someone to sell it for you. There are software publishers and distributors that specialize in this. The book *Programmer's Market*, published by Writers Digest Books, 9933 Alliance Road, Cincinnati, OH 45242, lists many of them. Another annual, Bowker/Bantam's *Complete Sourcebook of Personal Computing*, also lists software producers and distributors that may be interested in your product. Both of these resources are sold in most large bookstores.

A word of warning: Ideas are easy to copy. A shady company could reject your software product and use your original idea to write a set of programs for themselves.

Some of the major book publishers have entered the business of selling programs for the microprocessor. Here are a few of the largest:

McGraw-Hill Book Co.
1221 Avenue of the Americas
New York, NY 10020

IBM Personal Computer displayed at the first international scientific and computer exhibition held in the Shenzhen Special Economic Zone, a trade zone established by the People's Republic of China to promote economic development.

Prentice Hall Inc.
Route 9W
Englewood Cliffs, NJ 07632

Reader's Digest
Pleasantville, NY 10570

Simon & Schuster
1230 Avenue of the Americas
New York, NY 10020

Warner Publishers
666 Fifth Avenue
New York, NY 10103

A well-known software distributor is Softsel Computer Products, Inc., 546 North Oak St., Inglewood, CA. 90302. As a middleman between the manufacturer and the retailer, Softsel evaluates software, buys programs that it thinks will sell, and resells them to retailers.

Some large software producers like Microsoft Corporation, 10700 Northup, Bellevue, WA 98004, sometimes sell their products directly to retailers, bypassing distributors. IBM sells software packages through its company outlets; armed with its own huge sales force, Big Blue sells business software directly to its longtime friend, the large corporate customer.

If you have a truly lucrative software idea, companies like Electronic Arts of San Mateo, California, might promote you as one of their software "stars." With Apple Computer's co-founder, Steve Wozniak, on its board of directors, Electronic Arts "seeks out and signs, under royalty, top software designers to create programs for publication."

Many of their programmers now under contract are assembly language whizzes. According to Electronic Arts, the company is making a major investment in software tool technology, which will lead to a software development system for its artists. Electronic Arts says that for future machines its development system will provide an overwhelming advantage over techniques used today.

Electronics Arts sees today's entertainment software as "best described as shallow—of insufficient challenge, often boring after a few plays." The company believes such products will soon be rejected in favor of products that allow the consumer to explore and enjoy fully the powerful capabilities of the computer.

"The market," according to Electronic Arts, "is ready for a new kind of software—software in which software artists can imbue the best of their creative and technical skills, software that meets the individual's need to play, to be entertained, to explore, to discover, to satisfy curiosity, and to learn."

Electronic Arts sells directly to retailers. It packages its software products in distinctive album-like formats with eye-grabbing graphics and playing hints. To enhance computer awareness of its titles, it uses aggressive advertising and innovative merchandising techniques adapted from the book and record publishing industries.

The producers of its Talent Development Department may be looking for *your* brilliant software product. If they put you under contract, Electronic Arts promises "technical advice on target machines, user-interface design, software structuring, and other aspects of software production."

Electronic Arts lists such entertainment conglomerates as Warner Communications, Twentieth Century-Fox, and CBS as its competitors. The publisher notes that "the market will be large and diverse and will support a variety of approaches. Nonetheless, competition will be fierce, and not all the entrants will survive."

Computer companies come and go at an alarming rate. One day you read of the huge profits of the "Widget Co."; several months later its Profit and Loss Statement is bright red. If a product lacks differentiation, other businesses can move in with a similar service at a lower cost and squeeze a young company out of business.

In the past, many enterprising software entrepreneurs have formed a type of company known as a *computer service bureau.* Some of these have been extremely successful; others, unable to adjust to change, have failed. A service bureau sells turnkey software services; it develops complicated software to solve general or specialized business problems, runs the programs on its own or a rented mainframe or minicomputer, and delivers the output to the customer. Referred to as *batch processing*, this type of service is slowly being replaced as on-line terminals, microprocessors, and other in-house computers conquer the market.

Up-to-date service bureaus offer customers on-line services. Customers access the computer company's mainframe using video display terminals or personal computers. Some companies that began as service bureaus have evolved into *systems integrators.* They specialize in buying computers, terminals, printers, and other equipment and bundling these components together with extremely sophisticated systems and proprietary applications software to create a complete computer system with *networking* (data communications) capabilities.

For the future entrepreneurs among you, here is a true story of how one man founded a highly successful Texas software company. About eighteen years ago, way before microcomputers, a bright young IBM Service Bureau salesman dreamed of being an IBM sales manager. He targeted all his effort to reach that admirable goal. After a few years, his enormous dedication paid off. In 1969 he sold more computer services than any other IBM salesman in the U.S. For this, Big Blue made him a member of the IBM Golden Circle, a coveted honor.

Soon thereafter the salesman was summoned to the boss's office. With a firm pat on the back, the boss told him that he was to be promoted to sales manager in the nation's capital. Frowning, the young salesman's face dropped. Leave Houston, I can't do *that*! he thought. But he did—though not for long.

Within one year he was back in Texas—jobless. He had quit a top-paying managerial position with the world's most powerful computer company to start his own business, rather than leave his beloved city. His best friends shook their heads with doubt.

Luckily, the former IBMer had some outstanding assets: He obviously was a crack salesman, he was a natural though self-taught programmer/analyst, and most important, he believed in himself.

With no income and only enough savings to feed his family for one year, how did he buy a multimillion-dollar mainframe computer and an office building in which to house it? With the banker unwilling and his dad willing but unable to help, how did he hire programmers, systems analysts, salesmen, computer operators, and a gorgeous secretary to staff his company? The answer is—he *didn't*!

Instead, he did his own design and programming, sold his product himself, ran his programs on a rented computer on weekends and in the middle of the night, and drafted his wife to serve as his secretary and assistant programmer. Above all he remained optimistic!

Sixteen-hour workdays were the norm. How could anyone tolerate such a load? It was only possible because he loved what he was doing. How long did he continue to work those ridiculous hours under the mental strain that is inherent in the software business? Those of you with the entrepreneurial spirit will answer: "As long as it was necessary." When he finally roped his first cherished customer, he did more than keep him happy—he treated him like a god; after all, the customer was the tiny company's only reference!

Finally, the fragile "company" had enough customers to afford one bona fide employee. The young entrepreneur had reached a crucial crossroads: He suddenly was a leader of men. If he had been unable to develop managerial skills—fast—his fledgling software firm, unable to expand, would have died in infancy. Only as the leader of a winning team could he attract outstanding, dedicated professionals capable of turning the small company into a high-powered national corporation.

Do you see yourself in this young man's role? Perhaps *you* have that rare gift, the entrepreneurial spirit. Positive answers to the following questions might indicate that you do:

Do you have a burning desire to take the helm and run your own business?

Do you have an inventive mind?

Can you find new ways of solving other people's problems?

Can you bring your ideas to life in the real world?

Are you a builder and a creator?

Do you have driving energy?

Will you stick with a project long after your "sane" friends have relaxed in front of the TV?

Are you venturesome, at times almost fearless?

Will you take *carefully* thought-out risks?

Do you see opportunity where others see failure?

Can you adjust to continuous changes, such as technology-on-the-march?

Can you take setbacks without "throwing in the towel"?

Can you sell your ideas to others?

Youth does not seem to be a disadvantage to an entrepreneur. Consider the story of the founding of Microsoft Corporation by Harvard mathematics student Bill Gates and Honeywell assistant programmer Paul Allen.

According to Microsoft: "In 1974, MITS announced the release of the Altair, the first commercially available microcomputer, and Gates and Allen decided to try to develop the first high-level language for a microprocessor environment. They were successful!

"Together they developed enhanced versions of the BASIC language which eventually ran interchangeably on the Zilog Z-80, Mostek 6502, Intel 8086, Motorola 68000 and MC 6800, and the Zilog Z-8000 [chips]." After completing the initial releases of BASIC, Microsoft went on to develop other languages for microcomputers, and the line now includes operating systems, application tools, and entertainment packages.

Microsoft's success story skyrocketed when "in 1980, IBM began to go to outside sources to develop its own microcomputer. They went to Intel for the 8088 microprocessor, and to Microsoft for a new operating system. The system Microsoft designed for them, MS-DOS, has emerged as the dominant operating system for 8086 and 8088 microprocessor-based systems and is now being shipped with 96 percent of those systems that are sold."

Still under thirty years old, Bill Gates now presides over the privately held multimillion-dollar Microsoft Corporation.

Apple Computer also was founded by two young entrepreneurs. For those of you who are unfamiliar with the company's rags-to-riches story, here is the exciting account of its founding as given by the company:

"The history of Apple Computer begins in early 1976, when two young, self-made engineers collaborated on a small computing board for personal use. Steven P. Jobs, then 21, and Stephen G. Wozniak, then 26, took six months to design a prototype and 40 hours to build it. They soon had an order for 50 of their personal computers.

"With that first order in hand, they raised about $1,350 by selling a used Volkswagen van and a programmable calculator. They set up shop in Job's garage and soon were doing well enough to form Apple Computer Company, with Jobs as business manager and Wozniak as engineer. They named their computer and the company 'Apple,' because an apple represents the simplicity they were trying to achieve in the design and use of their computers.

"That first computer—sold in kit form to electronics hobbyists— was so successful that demand soon outstripped the capacity of Jobs' garage and overtaxed their capital. Believing they had a product with great commercial and social value, Jobs and Wozniak set out to find professional managers.

"Their first recruit was A. C. (Mike) Markkula, Jr., whom they met through a mutual friend. Markkula had successfully managed marketing in two semiconductor companies that had experienced dynamic growth—Intel Corporation and Fairchild Semiconductor.

"After researching the personal computer market and assessing Apple Computer's chances, the three men developed plans for acquiring the necessary capital, management expertise, technical innovation, software development, and marketing. Initial financing came from Markkula and a group of venture capitalists that included Venrock Associates and Arthur Rock and Associates. Apple Computer, Inc. was incorporated on January 3, 1977.

"Apple remained a private corporation until December 1980, when it made an initial public offering of 4.6 million shares of common stock. Apple has grown in seven years from a two-man operation to become an international corporation of more than 4,500 employees with annualized sales at the billion dollar rate."

UCS, Microsoft, and Apple were started by men under thirty years of age. If you are older, keep in mind that Thomas J. Watson, Sr.—angry because he had been fired by National Cash Register Company—founded IBM when he was forty.

Although software entrepreneurs work at a hectic pace, the successful ones seem to love what they do. One programmer/analyst/salesman, who is now president of his own company, admits that his work is his life. He also claims, however, that his sanity depends on his six weeks of vacation every year. The software business is tough.

This executive has traveled all over the world with his forty-five-pound briefcase in one hand and a coding pad in the other. Each day, while on vacation, he rises at five in the morning to do several hours worth of program design work.

Once, many years ago, he left his work at home. Without his programming for an entire week, the executive grew sullen and restless—the trip was a disaster. Ever since, his wife has refused to travel with him unless he takes his work along.

Is this entrepreneur stark raving mad? No! He loves his work. After all, it has paid for tens of thousands of dollars worth of vacations.

Chapter **IV**

Who Are the Software Creators?

With the continued miniaturization of computer circuits, the size and cost of computer hardware has dropped to the point where more of us have access to our own shiny machine. This, however, is just the beginning of our cost as new owners; the slot in our computer is software-hungry. If it is to play games with us, teach us, work for us, and communicate with other computers over data networks, our electronic marvel must be "fed" diskettes with detailed machine instructions stored on them. Since each of these specialized programs has to be developed, you can readily see why the high-tech revolution has created jobs by the thousands.

Says Hewlett-Packard President John Young: "Electronics now is a $230 billion industry, ranking seventh worldwide. By the turn of the century, it probably will be second only to health care in size." According to Young as quoted by the Stanford University News Service: The U.S. semiconductor industry may spend hundreds of millions to "jump clear over the next generation of technology..." Young is a Stanford University trustee.

TWENTY FASTEST-GROWING OCCUPATIONS, 1982–1995*

Occupation	Percent Growth in Employment
Computer service technicians	96.8
Legal assistants	94.3
Computer systems analysts	85.3
Computer programmers	76.9
Computer operators	75.8
Office machine repairers	71.7

Occupation	Percent Growth in Employment
Physical therapy assistants	67.8
Electrical engineers	65.3
Civil engineering technicians	63.9
Peripheral EDP equipment operators	63.5
Insurance clerks, medical	62.2
Electrical and electronic technicians	60.7
Occupational therapists	59.8
Surveyor helpers	58.6
Credit clerks, banking and insurance	54.1
Physical therapists	53.6
Employment interviewers	52.5
Mechanical engineers	52.1
Mechanical engineering technicians	51.6
Compression and injection mold machine operators, plastics	50.3

---

*1995 projections from the *Monthly Labor Review*, U.S. Bureau of Labor Statistics.

According to the U.S. Department of Labor: "Employment of programmers is expected to grow faster than the *average* for all occupations through the 1980's as computer usage expands, particularly in firms providing accounting, business management, and computer programming services, and in organizations involved in research and development."

Jobs for systems analysts are expected "to grow much faster than the average for all occupations" during the same period. Analysts will be needed to design everything from sophisticated accounting packages to computer-integrated manufacturing systems (CIM is discussed in Chapter VIII).

Computer scientists who graduated in the spring of 1984 started their new jobs at an average salary of $2,072 a month, estimates the Endicott Report, a salary survey produced by Northwestern University. This is approximately 30 percent higher than that for a graduate with a bachelor's degree in business. No wonder students are flocking to computer courses.

Keep in mind, however, that although the information industry is experiencing rapid growth, software-related jobs will account for only a small percentage of the *overall* labor force. In other words,

society will continue to have far more positions available for nurses than for systems analysts. In 1980, for example, 1,655,000 persons were employed as registered and practical nurses while 205,000 worked as systems analysts.

Only 3 percent of all employment in 1982 was in high-tech occupations, according to an analysis of several long-term labor forecasts by Russell W. Rumberger and Henry M. Levin of Stanford's Institute for Research on Educational Finance and Governance. While employment in high-tech jobs is expected to increase by 46 percent by 1995, it will still account for only about 6 percent of all new jobs in the economy, according to the study as reported by the Stanford University News Service.

Reports Bob Beyers of the News Service: "While employment of computer programmers is expected to increase more than 10 percent annually according to the Institute for Economic Analysis estimates, Rumberger and Levin believe this projection may be overstated because user-friendly software will increasingly allow computers to be used without programmers."

The software industry is a dynamic part of the economy, with places like Silicon Valley (San Jose, California), Boston, and Austin (Texas) serving as key high-tech centers. Across the country, from Washington to Chicago to Albuquerque to Los Angeles, computer-oriented companies are looking for software personnel. That is not to say, however, that the software labor market is without some soft spots, especially in certain geographical areas. You obviously should find more jobs working with computers in a prosperous urban area than in a small farming community. Even in large cities the job outlook changes constantly. For instance, Houston in the late 1970s was a city in search of programmers; today employers there are able to find software talent with much less effort.

Exactly who are these skilled professionals who teach computers to work for mankind? They are a dynamic group of well-trained specialists who have chosen to work in either the commercial or the scientific environment.

In business, they have a variety of titles after their names such as systems analyst, applications programmer, programmer/analyst, systems programmer (not to be confused with systems analyst), data communications specialist, or software engineer.

In the scientific community, physical scientists, computer scientists, mathematicians, and engineers serve as systems analysts; and technical programmers write the detailed instructions in one of the programming languages that tell the computer what to do.

Program developers specialize still further in that they usually become expert in either systems or applications software. Exactly what is *systems software?* When computer scientists use this term they usually mean the computer's all-powerful operating system, although they also may be referring to the *database management* system (electronic file control programs), the *data communications system* (network control programs), the *security software* (access control and encryption programs), or some other phase of executive software.

What is a computer's *operating system* (OS)? Huge complex technical manuals like the IBM System/370 *Principles of Operation*—jokingly called the "POO" book—are available from IBM and other hardware manufacturers that describe hardware-specific operating systems. In brief, however, a computer's OS is a set of extremely sophisticated programs that control the inner workings of the computer. Like the conductor of an orchestra, the operating system "runs the show." Passing control of the computer back and forth between various programs, it coordinates the operation of multiple programs concurrently (almost simultaneously). The OS also handles incoming (input) and outgoing (output) information from the external or peripheral devices (the TV-like terminals, disk drives, tape drives, and printers).

The operating system, which is supplied by the manufacturer, must be in place for the machine to function. You could say that these supervisory control programs *support* the applications programs. A computer delivered without its operating system will not run—period.

The *applications programs*, on the other hand, are used by the computer to solve a particular problem, such as keeping track of parts in a warehouse. Although you will be unable to execute an inventory control program without the appropriate applications software, the machine will still be "alive" and ready to work as long as the systems software is in place. These rather complicated concepts will become clearer to you as you read what each job entails. For now, just keep in mind that in computerese systems and applications programs are in two distinct categories.

Systems Analyst

One of the "big chiefs" in the software industry is the commercial *systems analyst*. Armed with knowledge of business and computers, he is a key man because he designs the computer software that tells

The IBM 3083 system complex, one of the processors in IBM's large-scale advanced-technology series.

the hardware (the physical machine) how to get a job done. Since he creates the master plans for software systems, he must have a comprehensive understanding both of the problems to be solved and of computer systems. This requires a strong background in business or information sciences or both, with expertise in some phase of accounting, economics, business management, or data processing.

In its 1984 *Computer Salary Survey and Career Planning Guide*, the professional recruiting firm Source edp puts the systems analyst's salary range from $23,000 to $58,000. The analyst's depth of knowledge, experience working with people, and heavy responsibilities make him a candidate for promotion into management, especially in companies that specialize in computer software.

What does the systems analyst do all day? He may begin work by planning the layout of all the input and display screens that will appear on the computer's TV-like terminals (cathode ray tubes with keyboards). He formats the output reports such as Profit and Loss Statements and designs specialized forms such as invoices or statements. He sets up the system's file structure and specifies record layouts, contents, and interrelationships. A computer record might contain someone's name, address, phone number, and account number.

A systems analyst may spend part of his day exchanging ideas with management, other experts, and customers. He depends on his personal communication skills to listen to his employer's problems and explain his ideas for their solution using a computer system. Once his design is approved by the executive offices, he must explain his plan in detail to the programming department. Since he usually has experience in programming—often he has worked his way up through the programming ranks—he understands the complexities of writing software.

A few systems analysts also are capable of making high-level *system configuration* recommendations involving the purchase of tens of thousands of dollars worth of computer hardware. System configuration is the way a group of machines such as the *central processing unit* (CPU or "mainbrain") and the *peripheral equipment* (such as the input/output or I/O devices) are set up to work together to form an entire interconnected computer system.

When considering the appropriate CPU for an installation, the systems analyst must choose from the myriad computer models that are available. The choice of peripheral equipment is equally difficult, for he has to determine what kinds of and how many disk drives, tape drives, printers, and CRTs (cathode ray tubes) fit his employer's needs.

The systems analyst must take into account an unbelievable number of complicated factors when configuring a computer system. Besides price and equipment dependability, the analyst has to consider the manufacturer's long-term viability and its reputation for hardware maintenance (repair of broken equipment) and support (advice). Excellence in these last two areas has been IBM's stepping-stone to greatness.

Of utmost importance to his hardware decisions is the question of software compatibility. Will his company's expensive library of existing programs run on the new machine? In five years, when the boss wants to upgrade again to the latest model, will the data processing department be able to move the company's valuable software to another new computer without the enormous cost of rewriting it.

Programs have to be continuously improved and updated, but the idea of completely redoing a huge software system in order to switch hardware causes high-level executives to shake in their boots. Some systems take years to develop; programming expense alone, to say nothing of management and clerical salaries, office space, and machine time, can run into the millions of dollars.

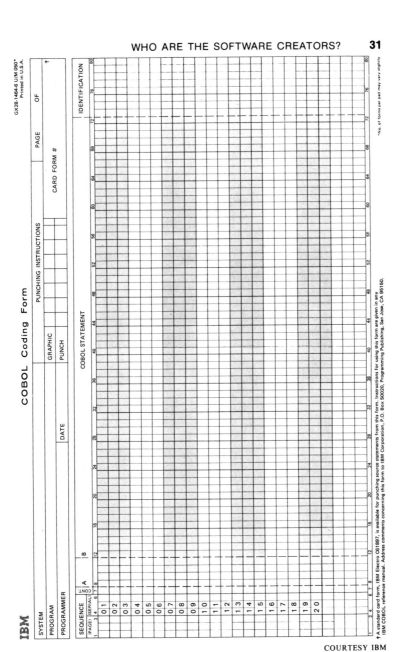

Fig. 4/1. *COBOL coding form.*

Suppose this same systems analyst works for a company that needs the facilities of an electronic *database* (a huge file of information stored digitally on computer disks). Suppose also that top management wishes its employees to be able to access this database instantly via a data communications network from various terminals and personal computers all over the U.S. To perform this minor miracle requires complicated database and data communications software. If our systems analyst is not extremely well versed in database management (DBM) and data communications (DC), he will have to consult an expert in those disciplines. (See the section on the *systems programmer*, below.)

Applications Programmer

Following the system design set out by the systems analyst, the *applications programmer* codes (writes in one of the programming languages) step-by-step directions that tell the computer how to do a series of tasks. In business, he may code all types of general purpose and custom programs such as general ledger, inventory control, and payroll packages.

Using a special coding pad (see Figure 4/1), he writes the program in a programming language that is suited for the job he wants the machine to do. He then types his work into the computer on the keyboard attached to a video display terminal (CRT). Every day more programmers are bypassing the coding pad step and composing programs at the keyboard.

In the past, keypunch operators typed the programmer's code into cards, using machines to make holes in cards that the computer's card reader could decode. On-line terminals have made this punch-card method of entering programs almost obsolete.

In business, the applications programmer usually is skilled in a language called COBOL (short for *CO*mmon *B*usiness *O*riented *L*anguage). The name of the language should tell you that it is specifically designed to handle business tasks such as updating files and preparing reports. Because COBOL resembles English, it is one of the easiest languages to read once you understand its basic concepts.

Programmers have to organize all of the intricate steps of a program into a logical and efficient form. Some programmers use *flow-charts* to do this (see Figure 4/2). Flowcharts use symbols to represent the sequence of decisions and the actions based on those decisions that the computer must take to solve the problem.

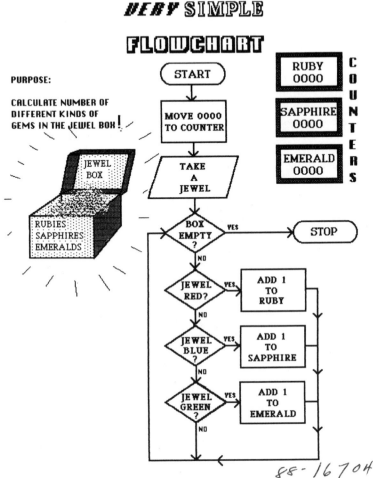

VERY SIMPLE

FLOWCHART

PURPOSE:

CALCULATE NUMBER OF
DIFFERENT KINDS OF
GEMS IN THE JEWEL BOX!

RUBY 0000

SAPPHIRE 0000

EMERALD 0000

C O U N T E R S

START

MOVE 0000
TO COUNTER

TAKE
A
JEWEL

BOX
EMPTY
? — YES → STOP

NO

JEWEL
RED? — YES → ADD 1 TO RUBY

NO

JEWEL
BLUE
? — YES → ADD 1 TO SAPPHIRE

NO

JEWEL
GREEN
? — YES → ADD 1 TO EMERALD

NO

JEWEL
BOX

RUBIES
SAPPHIRES
EMERALDS

88 - 16704

Fig. 4/2. *A flowchart drawn on a Macintosh computer by a ten-year-old child.*

One of the most important flowchart symbols is the diamond-shaped *decision symbol.* It is used when alternate paths based on changing conditions are possible. Look at the decisions in the diamond symbols in the sample flowchart. Examine also the rectangular *processing symbol.* Notice that the computer's processing functions are performed at this point.

Once the programmer has the logic organized either in a flow-chart or in his mind (many performers eventually find flowcharts unnecessary), he codes the program following the rules of his chosen programming language. Each type of language has its own set of strict conventions. If one of these rules is broken, the program will be rejected by the compiler.

The *compiler* is the language translator that changes the programmer's original source code into a series of binary instructions that the computer can understand. Only after the programmer has corrected every syntax error will the compiler translate the program into the *object* or machine *code*. This does *not* mean, however, that the computer has approved of the programmer's logic.

To determine if the program does what the designer intended it to do, the programmer must test his work, using test data that is representative of every possible type of information that will be input to the program. If his masterpiece puts out strange-looking reports containing farfetched figures, he will have to rethink his logic.

Obvious mistakes cause programmers less anxiety than hidden bugs that become apparent only under certain rarely occurring circumstances. (Errors were first nicknamed "bugs" when a moth

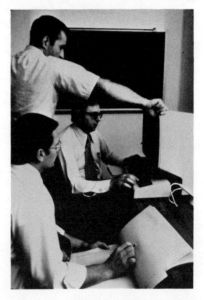

Programmers at work in front of a computer work station.

short-circuited one of the first computers.) A programmer, there-fore, must plan for every possible combination of factors so that he can create input test data to determine if his program will work under all conditions. Much to the programmer's embarrassment, undetected bugs often are discovered by angry customers.

A professional programmer must do more than write well-tested, error-free code; his programs also should follow standardized nam-ing conventions that facilitate understanding by other pro-grammers. For example, the programmers in the maintenance department will be required to make improvements and other changes to the original programmer's work. If his code is difficult to read because of illogical names and incomplete *documentation* (explanatory information), he will soon be out of a job. There are professional program documentors who relieve programmers of some of the work of making software understandable to nonpro-grammers and to the operations department. Documentation of applications programs may include an explanation of the goals of the program and descriptions of the various types of input, terminal screen layouts, record layouts, and output reports.

One programming manager summed up the importance of pro-gramming conventions and excellent documentation when he said: "Beautiful programs follow standardized conventions and are well documented with lots of explanations and remarks throughout the code. If one of my programmers rides off on his horse never to return, I don't want to have to throw away $50,000 worth of his projects because they look like Egyptian hieroglyphics."

As in most professions, rank also hath privilege in the program-ming profession. In business, there is a general hierarchy of applica-tions programmers. The entry-level programmer often begins in program maintenance. Under careful supervision, he is allowed to make simple improvements to an existing code.

After experience in maintenance, a programmer may be given the opportunity to code a program from scratch. If he consistently writes excellent software, he may be promoted to the position of group supervisor, where he will serve as the chief programmer and team leader in charge of several programmers. Following the design of the systems analyst, the group supervisor divides the program-ming job among his workers. As the project nears completion, he tests the group's effort to make certain that the programs do what the designer intended them to do.

Source edp puts the salary range for the commercial applications programmer and programmer analyst between $16,500 and $40,300 per year, depending upon responsibilities and experience.

Throughout this book software creators are referred to as programmer/systems analysts when a point can be applied to both. Think of a brilliant fifteen-year-old with a home computer who can design *and* write an original program; he is performing both systems analysis and programming functions. In small businesses and even in some larger companies, one person may do both jobs. Most analysts are also programmers, but the reverse may not be true; many programmers lack the background to do design work.

Systems Programmers

A few high-level applications programmers are able to make the big career switch to become systems programmers, or "bit twiddlers," as they are called in the industry. These highly skilled technical specialists are extremely knowledgeable in the operating systems and other programs that make the computer "tick." Although many of the "old-timers" (some of them are all of twenty-six years old) lack a degree in computer science, you may have to compete with CS graduates for systems programmer positions.

What do *systems programmers* do? You might say that they tinker with the "soul of the machine." Practically speaking, they install and implement the incredibly complicated systems software, especially the operating systems. During installation, for example, they customize these systems control programs to fit their particular computer's configuration.

Many systems programmers specialize in one of the mainframe operating systems. Some of the most famous are the IBM Disk Operating System (DOS), the DOS/VSE (VSE stands for virtual storage extended), or the MVS (multiple virtual systems), which is the operating system for large-scale computer installations.

Another operating system, AT&T's UNIX, is popular with minicomputer users, and versions are also available for microcomputers. Many of you probably have used one of the following microcomputer operating systems: Microsoft Corporation's MS-DOS, Digital Research's CP/M (Control Program/Monitor), or Apple DOS.

Since these systems control programs usually are written in one of the many *assembly languages*, systems programmers must be fluent in at least one version. Traditionally, the IBM assemblers have been *the* systems languages to know in business; that is especially true of DOS assembler.

Why is there more than one type of assembler language? The

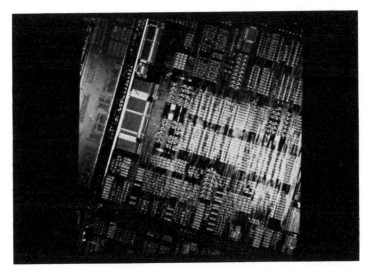

Advanced logic chips of the IBM 8150 processor.

answer is found by examining the heart of the computer—the chip. Computer chips vary: They are designed by different manufacturers, and they continually become outmoded by ever more powerful versions. Each new state-of-the-art chip architecture has its very own brand of assembler language.

The *chip*! Anointed the technological marvel of this century— exactly what is it? Capable of remembering instructions and making decisions, it is the "physical brain" of the computer. A tiny fleck of silicon with electronic circuitry embedded in it, the chip contains the *transistors* (off/on switches) that allow the computer to store information as strings of 0s (off—low voltage) and 1s (on—high voltage).

Since there are different types of these marvelous chips or *integrated circuits* (ICs), a proliferation of assembler languages has occurred (computers would lose their magic if they were simple). The Macintosh 32-bit superMICROcomputer, for example, is built around Motorola's MC68000 chip. Intel's 8088 microprocessor is at the core of IBM's first Personal Computer, and Intel's 80286 chip is the heart of the IBM AT "super PC."

Programming in any assembler language has been compared to "digging a grave with a teaspoon" because the programmer has to tell the computer every detailed step to take. For this reason, the assembler languages are referred to as low-level languages (as opposed to high-level languages such as COBOL). The advantage of any assembler language is that it allows a systems programmer to get close to the actual machine language so that he can manipulate the computer's *binary bits*, which store information and are represented by 0s or 1s. The disadvantage of any assembler language is that reading or writing an assembler program is a rather difficult and tedious experience.

In a high-level language such as COBOL, the *compiler* (translator program) assists the programmer by automatically generating more of the intricate machine instructions necessary to, for example, move data from one place to another. This frees the programmer to concentrate on the logic of the applications program—in itself no simple task.

Another language, called just plain C, is gaining in popularity with systems programmers. It was developed for the highly acclaimed UNIX operating system on a Digital Equipment Corporation minicomputer. Like the assembler languages, C facilitates computer bit manipulation. C, however, is a mid-level language and can accomplish a great deal with a few lines of code.

C receives praise from the academic community; it is easier to work with than assembler and produces programs that are portable (it will run on different types of computers with minimum changes).

Another programming language, PASCAL, which is a favorite teaching vehicle among universities, is used to introduce students to structured programming concepts and to systems programming. There are different versions of PASCAL, of which the Jensen and Wirth original definition is an important one. Apple Pascal, Macintosh Pascal, and Lisa Pascal will soon be well-known programming tools among many Apple computer users.

Systems programmers are in great demand with computer and peripheral manufacturers, computer service organizations, and data processing departments of large corporations. And they are highly paid. Salaries range from the low $20,000s at entry level to over $50,000 with experience.

A few systems programmers specialize in database management systems (DBMS) or data communications (DC), sometimes referred to as *teleprocessing* (TP). Simply put, *database management systems* handle database organization and maintenance; they let multiple users *concurrently* (almost simultaneously) read, write, and modify data on electronic files stored on hard (as opposed to floppy) disks. DBMS make such problems as file "overflow" transparent to the end-user.

Data communications specialists work with the teleprocessing software, which facilitates remote interaction ("talk" between the user and the system) with a database and with other computers or terminals. The word *teleprocessing* was derived from two words: TELEcommunications and data PROCESSING. TP stands for transmission of data to a remote site, often a video terminal.

Why are these specialties so hot? Obviously, one reason is that there are many more computer cursors blinking around the world today to be linked together. The proliferation of microcomputers has created more opportunity for computer "conversation" between these machines and powerful, mass-storage mainframes and minicomputers.

Another reason why communications experts are on personnel managers' "most wanted" lists is the horrendous lack of standardization that exists in the relatively new data communications industry. In other words, there is a confusing multiplicity of computer terminals and models, operating systems, databases, and communications protocols (sets of conventions that govern the flow of data between computers).

A company may wish, for example, to set up a network of several hundred *asynchronous* (binary data sent at random time intervals) microcomputers connected to an IBM mainframe that "speaks" *synchronously* (binary data transmitted and received at a fixed rate: the sender and receiver are synchronized). Special software is required to handle these conflicting protocols.

Microsoft Corporation's co-founder William H. Gates spoke of some of the difficulties of tying personal computers to mainframes in a news release entitled: "The Future of Software Design." According to Gates, "One of the major issues that software developers need to address is [this] growing interest in tying personal computers into mainframes. Because of the significant differences among mainframes, this is no simple matter. Mainframes—even those made by the same vendor—have different operating systems. The IBM S/370 architecture [a workhorse of business] alone has at least six major operating environments, and within each of those, multiple databases. Creating the software that will allow a personal computer to tie into such a machine will not be a trivial task.

"The problem is not simply tying two machines together. We've already done that: We have software that will turn the personal computer into a terminal, ignoring its local intelligence.

"The difficulty is to create a method of tying the two together that will allow automatic database query. The user should not, for example, have to know JCL [Job Control Language] to access data from the mainframe. Nor should he need to learn a complex set of command structures. Rather, he should be able to query data anywhere in the system and have the system itself use its intelligence to retrieve that data. In fact, the way the data was initially described in the dictionary should tell the system where to go to get it—whether to go, for example, to the mainframe, to CompuServe, or to Dow Jones. Resolving this software issue will not be easy, but it must be accomplished: The increasing use of personal computers in large organizations makes this a central concern today."

Busy end-users, whether they be housewives, scientists, or executives, demand easy transparent access to this "electronic universe." If, for example, a chemical engineer wishes to query a remote database of chemical abstracts, he obviously does not want to concern himself with how the computer software will get the information to him. It is the job of data communications programmers and managers, who are familiar with networking configurations and protocols, to provide that facility.

In homes and businesses across the country, personal computer owners already have the option of connecting their PCs to public databases such as The Source, Dow Jones News/Retrieval Service, and CompuServe. These information utilities, as they are sometimes called, are accessed via networks such as Tymshare's Tymnet and GTE's Telenet.

How many years will pass before the over eighty million volumes of the Library of Congress will be on-line? Who would dare hazard a guess! A small step in that direction, encyclopedic databases already are in operation.

One of the most famous is called *Dialog*, of Dialog Information Service, Inc., a subsidiary of Lockheed Missile and Space Corporation, 3460 Hillview Avenue, Palo Alto, CA 94304. Originally developed for NASA, it offers a diverse array of knowledge, everything from an International Software Directory of mini and microcomputer programs to a Career Placement Registry.

Private electronic libraries also already exist in business and industry; many more are on corporate drawing boards. Employees with access to specially equipped "intelligent" terminals like the

IBM 3270 series are able to *download* (accept data from the central computer) information to their remote machines from the company's private database. After manipulating the data to their satisfaction (some people call this work), they *upload* their results back to the mainframe's massive files.

The national on-line service at Universal Computer Systems, Inc., is a classic example of a private network. Created in the mid-1970's, Part-Net offers automobile dealers access to instantly updated parts inventory information from on-site terminals in dealerships. Using dedicated phone lines, UCS customers are connected to a huge distributed database, a portion of which is located at the central site in Texas and part of which is on disks at individual car dealers all over the country.

Much of the systems software that already has been written is described in a technical book called the *ICP Systems Software Directory*, published by International Computer Programs, Inc. Of its over 600 pages, 134 pages are devoted to database management and teleprocessing. The supplier/product index lists the companies that sell each system; such software houses are potential buyers of systems programmer talent. This resource, which is *not* easy reading, can be found in computer libraries.

Still in its infancy, the data communications industry is poised for takeoff. And you may be needed to give it the final push. As of 1984, Source edp places salaries of database specialists between $21,700 and $53,800 and data communications programmers and analysts between $22,800 and $48,300, depending on experience.

Another interesting software specialty involves the protection of information by building the software tools that provide for data integrity and security. Such programs guard extremely valuable electronic files against accidental and intentional harm and deny unauthorized disclosure or falsification of sensitive records.

One way of keeping the meaning of data out of the reach of criminals and spies is to use *algorithms* (a sequence of formulas) to encrypt it into a cipher (incomprehensible code). This method can be used to secure the confidentiality of information as it is transmitted over telecommunications networks. Encryption software specialists encrypt (encode) and decrypt (decode) data transmitted between and stored by computers. A privileged user is provided with a cryption key to add and retrieve data to and from the database.

The programs that protect electronic information often are written in assembler language. Skilled systems programmers who are knowledgeable in data security techniques are pursued by large banks and oil companies to create user-friendly but criminal-unfriendly protection systems. The military also has great interest in this specialty.

Systems Software Designer

A few of you may aspire to be a *systems software designer*. As one data processing executive puts it: "A systems designer is at the pinnacle of the programming profession." This technical guru of the software industry designs the omnipotent operating systems and other indispensable programs that the systems programmers implement.

The systems software designer advises others on software architecture and development. You are likely to find him with an *IBM Systems Journal* tucked under his arm; he may even have written one of its scholarly articles. He has enormous influence in the computer industry even though his profession accounts for a tiny percentage of the total number of software specialists.

What kind of educational background does he have? Usually he has an undergraduate degree, a master's, or even a PhD in computer science; however, he may be a "genius" with years of systems programming experience and no degree at all. Obviously, the main ingredient of his success is mastery of systems software.

Management Information Consultant

Another potentially rewarding career opportunity is that of a *management information consultant*. As this type of professional you might, for example, work for a large accounting firm or computer manufacturer that serves as an adviser to clients in the area of information handling. Depending on your expertise, you could offer your services to an insurance company, a bank, a high technology firm, or a manufacturing company.

Arthur Andersen & Co. has the largest consulting practice in the world. Says the accounting firm: "We act as the liaison between managers who may not have sufficient knowledge of advanced technological systems, and information processing professionals who may lack exposure to the broader business environment."

The company gives this example of consulting work for a multinational bank: "After establishing objectives and interviewing management, you would identify the information needed to manage their business and to serve their customers. You could then help plan hardware and software strategies, define the scope of the required information systems and review your work with client management to gain approval."

As a management information consultant, your knowledge of business practices and computer systems will be your product. Consequently, you will need solid academic credentials in one of the following disciplines: business, management information systems, computer science, economics, engineering, finance, marketing, or mathematics. A Master of Business Administration (MBA) is an excellent educational background if you wish to crack into the consulting business with a firm like Arthur Andersen.

Independent Contract Programmer

Would you relish the "freedom" to work at home with your baby sleeping in its crib and your dog at your feet? Once you are an experienced programmer or systems analyst, you will have the option of working as an *independent contract programmer* for an independent software organization (ISO)—perhaps your own one-person shop!

Although as a free-lance programmer you will be able to set your own hours, you also must find your own work and provide for your own benefits. Or you can turn to a temporary service broker who, for a fee, will find you a programming project.

If you choose to work as a contract programmer, you will have a definite advantage if you are competent in a specific applications area or if you are familiar with a specialized type of hardware. A typical assignment may last one or two years, with pay depending on your professional reputation and the difficulty of the job.

In November 1983 the Independent Computer Consultants Association (ICCA) published a survey showing that the "typical member of ICCA is about thirty-nine years old, a college graduate, and a recently converted entrepreneur."

According to the survey, two thirds are lone-professional businesses. The average number of professionals per firm was 2.3 persons while the average gross income per business was $139,000, and the average gross income per professional was $61,000. These findings emerged from a national survey of ICCA's members, of which 32 percent responded (see the accompanying tables for further details).

INDEPENDENT COMPUTER CONSULTANTS ASSOCIATION
Demographics as of November 1983

Table 1

	Count	Number of Professionals	Gross Income	Gross Income Per Professional
All Returns	355	2.3	139,000	61,000
East	115	2.1	140,000	60,000
Central	120	2.7	161,000	60,000
West	117	2.0	119,000	62,000
Chapters	304	2.3	145,000	62,000
Non-Chapters	48	2.2	97,000	55,000
Boston	17	1.8	82,000	39,000
Chicago	28	2.5	144,000	57,000
Connecticut	13	2.2	187,000	65,000
Detroit	16	2.3	105,000	47,000
Houston	15	3.8	325,000	103,000
Los Angeles	27	2.5	192,000	72,000
New York/ New Jersey	53	2.3	150,000	66,000
Northern California	55	1.5	77,000	59,000
Washington, DC	17	2.4	197,000	75,000
Other Chapters	63	2.5	142,000	55,000
One Professional	201	1.0	65,000	65,000
Multiprofessional	149	4.0	241,000	54,000

Scientific Software Developers

Some of the future scientists and engineers among you will be tomorrow's *scientific* software innovators. Armed with specialized education, software developers have made the computer an invaluable scientific tool. In fact, whole platoons of machines have invaded every technical discipline. Computer graphics programs, for example, assist research chemists in 3-D molecular modeling and engineers in automotive and aircraft design. Expert (computer) systems from the artificial intelligence (AI) community prospect for minerals and attempt to diagnose everything from human diseases to faults in the earth. (See Chapter VII for more on AI.)

Table 2

	Count	Radius (in miles)	Age (average)	Education (average years)	% Female (of CEO)
All Returns	355	126	39	17	13
East	115	86	39	17	14
Central	120	195	38	16	8
West	117	94	39	17	16
Chapters	304	106	39	17	14
Non-Chapters	48	251	38	17	6
Boston	17	73	39	17	0
Chicago	28	148	37	17	14
Connecticut	13	94	43	17	17
Detroit	16	66	36	16	12
Houston	15	242	37	16	7
Los Angeles	27	120	41	17	22
New York/ New Jersey	53	65	38	17	15
Northern California	55	81	38	17	19
Washington, DC	17	117	38	18	24
Other Chapters	63	126	40	16	8
One Professional	201	107	39	17	16
Multi-professional	149	152	38	17	9

In the scientific community degreed physical scientists, computer scientists, mathematicians, and engineers design these scientific systems, and technical programmers write the code in one of the assembly languages, FORTRAN, PASCAL, PL/1, C, ADA, LISP, or APL, to name a few.

Historically, FORTRAN (short for *for*mula *tran*slator) has been *the* language suited to "crunching numbers" at scientific installations. Originally developed by IBM for this purpose, FORTRAN source statements resemble mathematical notation. For example, the plus (+) or minus (–) symbol tells the computer to add or subtract and the asterisk (*) indicates multiplication. Since FORTRAN is a high-level language, the programmer can ignore machine functions and concentrate on the problem to be programmed. The FORTRAN compiler accepts complex formulas and algebraic expressions and translates them into binary machine language processing routines.

The following is a simple example of a FORTRAN statement:

$$ATOT = ATOT + B$$

This says to the computer: "Add the number called B to an amount called ATOT and store the result in the address where ATOT was stored."

In an effort to standardize the software written for the U.S. Department of Defense, DOD commissioned the development of a new language called ADA. Only time will tell if it can fulfill its weighty mission as a substitute for FORTRAN.

Software Engineers

Many of you may choose to be *software engineers*. These special-

The IBM 5080 graphic system—a designer's dream come true. Scientists and engineers can create high-resolution color graphic designs with the aid of the IBM 5080 and the appropriate software.

ists "design, code, check out, and release specific products," says one large computer manufacturer. "Projects range across our entire product spectrum from developing high-level language compilers and interpreters to subsystem development to market application. The position of CAD [computer-aided design] software engineer can include systems applications design, developing and supporting circuit layout design algorithms and systems, designing polycell LSI/VLSI chips, verifying designs, and supporting users in graphics, data structures and interfaces, and communications."

According to Source edp: "Manufacturers of personal computers, mini- and mainframe computers, robotics, CAD/CAM [computer-aided design/computer-aided manufacturing] and office automation systems are potential employers or software engineers. To find employment in this field, you probably will need a computer science or engineering degree. The salary range is from $21,000 to $43,000 per year." See Chapter VIII for further discussion of CAD/CAM.

Chapter V

High School—A Time to Seek Out the Target

The greatest legacy, perhaps the only real legacy we can leave our children is fully developed intellects.

We must turn our schools into places of learning. There is only one real issue—will the public support these changes?

Public schools reflect society. At a time when pleasure seeking and instant gratification are in vogue with both adults and children, and strong parental involvement with children is missing with roughly half of the three million children in our public [Texas] schools, are we going to ask our children to cut back on video games, television, video music and to cease leaving school early to make money to pay for cars? Will we ask them to work, toil and persevere—to take the difficult courses, not the soft electives—to learn? This will be a big change from the world of play that our public schools have become in many places across the State.

> H. Ross Perot
> Founder of
> Electronic Data Systems Corporation

For a brief moment, picture yourself speeding down a lonely country highway toward an unknown destination. Streaking past your peripheral vision are innumerable side roads branching off in every direction. At "Porsche" speed, once you have missed a turn it is exceedingly difficult to turn back.

If you are in high school, you may be bypassing crucial educational junctions that could have profound impact on your life's work. Lost opportunities provided by a free public education even at the junior high level are recovered only at considerable cost in time and money.

The 4381 system complex, one of IBM's powerful mid-range computer systems.

Much more than a plan metal box, this is a powerful mid-range IBM 4361 processor.

Every fork in your high school curriculum represents a decision—either active or passive. What you do *not* do will have great impact on your future career. Subjects missed at this point may be key stepping-stones later for admission to a desired college, a major, or a profession.

Since you cannot fast-forward your life in order to judge your current academic decisions, why not keep your educational and career options open by making the best possible grades in a *broad* range of subjects. At the same time, you can emphasize courses that are of particular interest for your future profession. By building a solid academic foundation in secondary school, you can target yourself toward the exciting career of your dreams.

Why is it important to get a strong *general* education if you know that you want to be, for example, a systems programmer? The answer is that as the software frontier advances and job definitions change, you will need the *flexibility* that comes with diverse knowledge. The ability to adapt to the unknown future is especially vital in the computer industry, where technology leaps ahead at breakneck speeds and last year's hottest product is tossed in next year's circular file.

Says H. Ross Perot in an important speech on education: "In a world driven by rapid change, we will not be able to prepare our children for specific jobs. We must provide them with a classic education. We must teach them to think, and adapt to a rapidly changing world."

"What defines and limits a career is the individual's *ability to learn throughout life*," says a Panel on Secondary School Education for the Changing Workplace sponsored by the Committee on Science, Engineering, and Public Policy, a joint committee of the National Academy of Sciences, National Academy of Engineering, and Institute of Medicine. "Technology will change, businesses will change, the content of a given job will change, and one's employer will change. What will never change is the need to adapt to new opportunities..."

"A person who knows how to learn is one well grounded in fundamental knowledge and who has mastered concepts and skills that create an intellectual framework to which new knowledge can be added," says the Stanford University News Service, reporting on the panel on education.

A broad high school education will pour the foundations upon which to build this "intellectual framework" as well as provide an opportunity for you to access your possible career interests.

Although even those will change over the years, first-time exposure to new areas of study at the secondary school level should help you answer questions like the following:

Do you excel at mathematics?

Do you love science courses?

Are you fascinated by computers?

Do you like to write?

Do you enjoy business courses?

Do you like to speak in public?

Are you persuasive?

Are you a scholar?

Your answers may lead to pivotal career questions such as:

Do you want to create or sell the programs that make computers come alive?

To learn to do this, what courses should you take and what books and periodicals should you read while you are in high school?

Will a college degree open the doors of the computer industry for you?

How can you pay college expenses?

Do you wish to specialize in commercial or scientific software?

Which of the following college majors should you pick?
    Computer Science
    Management Information Systems
    Information Science
    Information Systems
    Computer Information Systems
    Data Processing and Analysis
    Applied Mathematics
    Mathematical Sciences
    Computer Engineering
    Electrical Engineering
    Accounting

Economics
Finance
Marketing
Business Management
or some other specialty

What exciting opportunities will be available to you if you earn a master's degree or a PhD?

Do these and other majors prepare you for the careers mentioned earlier in this book?

Will a two-year associate degree prepare you to be a programmer?

Is it still possible to get a job and work your way up the software career ladder with only a high school diploma?

The above questions are considered in detail throughout this and the following chapters.

Ideally, your secondary education should provide you with more than a surface knowledge of computers so that you can make intelligent decisions about whether you wish to become a software professional before you start your post-high school education.

I recently talked with a bright young data processing graduate of a major university who was seeking his first job. I asked him what sort of position he hoped to find.

"Anything that does not involve programming," he replied with a long face. "I do not want to spend the rest of my life writing code. In fact, I really don't know what I want to do."

If he had had greater exposure to programming in high school, perhaps he would have discovered that he disliked writing code *before* he majored in data processing, which emphasizes computer languages along with business courses.

According to Ruth Milburn, Manager of the Information Project, Europe-Africa Division, Esso Exploration, Inc., an affiliate of EXXON: "The *ideal* secondary education would offer apprentice programs where students could spend several hours a day at a computer center."

Before EXXON, or any company, can hire you to "lay hands on" one of its multimillion-dollar computers, you will require a great deal of training. For this reason, Ruth Milburn would like to see you have the opportunity to assess your interest in computers as early as high school.

There are opportunities for a young person to learn about computers outside the high school classroom. Some colleges, for example, offer evening introductory computing classes as well as high-quality academic computer summer camps for the serious high school computer student.

According to Dr. Ken Kennedy, Professor of Mathematical Sciences and Chairman of the Committee for Computer Sciences at Rice University, Rice offers a three-week summer camp for a few outstanding high school students, where participants learn about microprocessors and how to program in PASCAL. The program is run by the Department of Computer Science in conjunction with the Office of Continuing Studies. If you live near a college, you might consider taking a similar course.

Many community colleges and family summer computer camps offer low-key introductory courses in BASIC, LOGO, and PASCAL where you can at least get your hands on a microprocessor. The quality and content of these classes vary greatly; it is time well spent to research each program before you invest your money. In a good one you will learn to *write* video games rather than *play* them.

You might even consider a computer tutor, perhaps a high school programming whiz, a university computer science student, a teacher, or even a systems analyst or programmer. One ambitious freshman gained access to a home computer and "free" advice by offering to do yard work for a neighbor who was a systems programmer.

One way to meet other people who are interested in computers is to join your high school computer club or a user group. Some of the computer retail stores listed in the Yellow Pages may have names of local clubs in your area. Bowker/Bantam's 1984 *Complete Sourcebook of Personal Computing*, which is found in some libraries and bookstores, lists 1,100 computer clubs and user groups in the U.S. and Canada.

A part-time or summer job working for any company with a computer installation would give you a firsthand opportunity to observe computer professionals at work. If you are extraordinarily lucky, you might land a computer operator's job, but even a maintenance or clerical position will provide you with a close-up glimpse of the industry. In fact, any high school work experience properly executed will improve your future résumé.

IBM Education offers a whole range of courses for its business customers. Although most of these programs are prohibitively expensive for most individuals, the company's self-study COBOL programming course is available for $60. According to the Catalog of IBM Education (April 1984, published by Science Research Associates, Inc., Information Systems Education Division, 155 North Wacker Drive, Chicago, IL 60606), this course teaches novices to program in ANS COBOL. Published by Mike Murach & Associates, the ANS COBOL Series [SS069] begins with an entry-level programming textbook entitled *Structured ANS COBOL I* [SR20-4683]. SRA lists its *Programming Fundamentals Series* (32310), or *equivalent* knowledge, as a prerequisite for the COBOL series. Complete with video cassettes, this fundamental course, which is designed for IBM's corporate customers rather than high school students, is not cheap.

There are, however, numerous computer books available at college libraries and bookstores, commercial bookstores, and public libraries that teach computer literacy, data processing, computer science, and various programming languages on an introductory and advanced level. Remember to check the date of publication to make certain that it is not ancient history.

McGraw-Hill's annotated 1984 *Computer Catalog* lists many new offerings. Some bookstores may have the catalog, or write: Computer Marketing Services-1, McGraw-Hill Book Company, Princeton-Hightstown Road, Hightstown, NJ 08520. The publisher's college division also puts out a catalog called *Engineering*, which lists and describes books written by college professors and others in engineering and computer science. The following is a sampling of books from these catalogs that may be of interest to some of you.

The McGraw-Hill Encyclopedia of Electronics
   & Computers
The staff of the McGraw-Hill Encyclopedia of Science
   and Technology
Found in the reference section of some libraries
1983   CC 07-045487-6

Introduction to Business Data Processing, 2d ed.
L. S. Orilia
1982   CC 07-047835-x

Schaum's Outline of Introduction to Computer Science
Including 300 solved problems
   CC 07-055195-2

Armchair BASIC
An absolute beginner's guide to programming in BASIC
A. Fox and D. Fox
Osborne
1983   CC931988-92-6

Schaum's Outline of Programming with BASIC, 2d ed.
1982   CC 07-023855-3

Structured COBOL, 2d ed.
A. S. Philippakis and L. J. Kasmier
1981   CC 07-049801-6

Schaum's Outline Series
Programming with Structured COBOL
L. Newcomer
1984   CC 07-037998-x

PASCAL
G. Bellford and C. L. Liu
1984   CC 07-038138-0

A First Course in Computer Programming with PASCAL
A. M. Keller
1982   CC 07-033508-7

Computer Graphics
A Programming Approach
S. J. Harrington
1983   CC 07-026751-0

Discrete Mathematics
Seymour Lipschutz, Temple University
1976   0-07-037981-5

Addison-Wesley Publishing Company, Inc., Reading, MA 01867, also has an annotated 1984-85 *Computer Books and Software Catalog.* Here is a selection of its books.

Computers and Data Processing, 2d ed.
H. L. Capron and B. K. Williams
1984   0-8053-2214-0

Information Processing Systems: An Introduction to Modern Computer-Based Information Systems, 2d ed.
William S. Davis
1981   0-201-03183-3

BASIC and the Personal Computer
Thomas A. Dwyer and Margot Critchfield
1978   0-201-01589-7

Writing Structured COBOL Programs
David Johnson
1985   0-201-11591-3

COBOL: A Primer and a Programmer's Guide
Ross A. Overbeek and Wilson E. Singletary
1985   0-201-16310-1

Problem Solving and Structured Programming in FORTRAN,
2d ed.
Frank L. Friedman and Elliot B. Koffman
1981   0-201-02461-6
        0-201-02465-9 Student Workbook

Programming Concepts and Problem Solving:
An Introduction to Computer Science Using PASCAL
Peter B. Linz
1983   0-8053-5710-6

An Introduction to Operating Systems, rev. ed.
Harvey M. Deitel
1984   0-201-14501-4

Experts disagree as to which languages you should learn at the high school level, or any level for that matter. Of course, BASIC and LOGO are great for beginners and kids, but they are unsuited to most business applications.

Businesses and government agencies loaded down with mountains of programming projects hope that you will become an expert COBOL programmer. But four-year colleges, worried about your future fifteen years down the road, want to give you an in-depth theoretical knowledge of computing in addition to language skills.

If you are headed for a bachelor's degree, remember that college programs introduce students to programming with PASCAL. The College Board considers Jensen and Wirth's PASCAL: *User Manual and Report*, 2d ed. (published by Springer-Verlag, New York), to be the standard for PASCAL for its Advanced Placement Examination.

According to Dr. Kennedy of Rice University: "Colleges offer PASCAL to students because it is an excellent vehicle for teaching programming and the ideas of programming. PASCAL has a simplicity of design and an efficiency for compilation and for interpretation that makes it very suitable for teaching programming concepts. Students taught to program in PASCAL can learn quite easily to program in other languages."

With hundreds of lines of COBOL to maintain, one Houston executive says with a scowl: "I have been hiring COBOL programmers for fifteen years. During this time the universities have emphasized other languages like FORTRAN and PASCAL. The colleges say that once you learn PASCAL you can quickly learn COBOL or any other language. But I need crack COBOL programmers who really know what they are doing—this takes time."

I asked Professor Kennedy if he thought that COBOL would continue to be the predominant applications language of business.

"That is not a subject that I can predict," he replied. "I suspect that COBOL will survive as long as its usage is supported by a number of businesses and by the U.S. government for certain kinds

COURTESY NASA

An IBM 360-75, a workhorse of the past. Overall view of computer installation that was formerly in the Mission Control Center at the Johnson Space Center, part of the equipment of the Software Development Laboratory.

of applications. I think, however, that systems used by business will be written in many other languages. I do not predict COBOL's death, nor do I predict that it will dominate the field.

"A primary value of COBOL is that they [COBOL developers] have spent a good deal of time working on the facilities for the management of data on secondary storage, and there is a set of extensions of COBOL for the management of databases. I suspect that programs will continue to be written in COBOL for that reason."

The future systems programmers among you, who have taken the Advanced Placement Computer Science Course in high school and claim to be PASCAL, COBOL, or FORTRAN whizzes, may wish to learn IBM System/370 Machine Language. (At the time of writing, the System/370 series of computers is one of the leading machine architectures used in business.) This family of computers includes not only the IBM System/370 series and the IBM 4300 series, but the IBM 303X and 308X series as well as the now-outdated IBM System/360 models. The following extremely technical Addison-Wesley book teaches S/370 assembler programming:

Assembler Language Programming:
The IBM System/370 Family, 3d ed.
George W. Struble
1984   0-201-07815-5

If you want to learn to "twiddle" the bits of your microprocessor, books are available that teach professionals to program each chip using the appropriate assembly language. With the birth of every new chip architecture, a publication is written to teach software specialists how to program it. Conversely, as a chip becomes outmoded, its assembler eventually is no longer used.

Two publishers of this type of highly technical book are: *Sybex* (2344 Sixth Street, Berkeley, CA 94710) and Osborne/McGraw-Hill (2600 Tenth Street, Berkeley, CA 94710). For example, if you are determined to program the 68000 supermicro chip (the heart of the Macintosh), the *68000 Microprocessor Handbook and 68000 Assembly Language Programming* book published by McGraw-Hill will give you a fighting chance.

For the scholars among you, who wish to research the latest scientific papers written on a particular computer-oriented subject, there is a resource in the reference section of many college libraries to help you: the *Computer and Information Systems Abstracts*

Journal, published by Cambridge Scientific Abstracts, 5161 River Road, Bethesda, MD 20816. Published monthly, it contains abstracts or outlines of research papers. The first section of each update consists of abstracts on computer software. Since every volume is indexed by subject, it is easy to locate information. For example, I looked up "artificial intelligence" and found at least thirty-five entries.

The computer trade magazines and journals are a great way to learn about the software industry, and the number of publications from which to choose is mind-boggling. To help busy computer professionals see at a glance many of the articles written each month, a biweekly reference guide called *Computer Contents* prints the table of contents of trade periodicals. Published by Management Contents, 2265 Carlson Drive, Northbrook, IL 60062, a single copy costs $4.00 For a fee subscribers can receive photocopies of the full text of articles of interest.

The Association for Computing Machinery, 11 West 42nd Street, New York, NY 10036, publishes the most comprehensive annual listing of literature on computing, *ACM Guide to Computing Literature*. It names 14,000 current scientific books, papers, and reports. This resource can be found in some college computer science libraries and large industrial computer libraries.

The following are important trade magazines and newspapers that future computer professionals should read faithfully. You can find them in public and college libraries, computer retail stores, and bookstores.

Byte
McGraw-Hill
P.O. Box 328
Hancock, NH 03449

Datamation
Technical Publishing Co.
875 Third Avenue
New York, NY 10022

Computerworld
CW Communications/Inc.
Box 880
375 Cochituate Road
Framingham, MA 01701

PC The Independent Guide to IBM Personal Computers
Ziff-Davis Publishing Co.
One Park Avenue
New York, NY 10016

PC World
555 De Haro St.
San Francisco, CA 94107

Technology Review
Massachusetts Institute of Technology
Room 10-140
Cambridge, MA 02139

High Technology
High Technology Publishing Corporation
P.O. Box 2810
Boulder, CO 80322

Macworld
The Macintosh Magazine
Subscription Department
P.O. Box 20300
Bergenfield, NJ 07621

The Wall Street Journal
Dow Jones & Company, Inc.
　Eastern Edition
　22 Cortlandt Street
　New York, NY 10007

　Western Edition
　220 Battery Street
　San Francisco, CA 94111

　Midwest Edition
　200 West Monroe Street
　Chicago, IL 60606

　Southwest Edition
　1233 Regal Row
　Dallax, TX 75247

Another excellent source of information about the computer
industry is the Institute for Certification of Computer Professionals
(ICCP), 35 East Wacker Drive, Chicago, IL 60601, and its Charter

Member Societies. The ICCP "is a nonprofit organization established for the purpose of testing and certifying knowledge and skills of computing personnel." The Institute offers a Certificate in Computer Programming (CCP) examination and a Certificate in Data Processing (CDP) examination to computer professionals. A person who has passed the CCP test may sign his name: John Doe, CCP. Once he passes both exams, he has earned the right to this signature: John Doe, CCP, CDP.

Candidates who take the Certificate in Computer Programming examination are "expected to possess a reading knowledge of FORTRAN, COBOL, PL/1, and an assembly language." The Certificate in Data Processing examination is designed as a "method to measure knowledge appropriate to the management of data processing."

The ICCP tests may be of interest to high school students only in that they provide outlines of the content of professional exams in the industry, including sample questions and a comprehensive list of relevant reference books. A reprint of the outlines is given at the end of this chapter. Although the influence of the ICCP is increasing, a great many extremely successful software professionals have been too busy creating products to take these tests.

According to the ICCP, it does not publish a Review Manual for the CDP examination, nor does it officially endorse any manual now in print. However, in case you do not have access to a comprehensive data processing library, the following are review manuals listed by ICCP:

CDP Review Manual/
  A Data Processing Handbook, 3d ed.
Lord and Steiner, through International Thompson, $29.95
7625 Empire Drive
Florence, KY 41042

Also available through
Van Nostrand & Reinhold
135 West 50th Street
New York, NY 10020

One Thousand and One Questions and Answers
  to Help You Prepare for the CDP Exams
K. Lord
Q.E.D. Information Sciences, Inc., $18.50
P.O. Box 181
Wellesley, MA 02181

CDP Exam Guide
DPMA—Washington, D.C. Chapter
John Wiley & Sons, Inc., $16.95
605 Third Avenue
New York, NY 10158

Some of the ICCP charter member societies also may help you gather information about the industry. Following is an annotated listing:

INSTITUTE FOR CERTIFICATION OF COMPUTER PROFESSIONALS

Charter Member Societies

ACM: The *Association for Computing Machinery* was founded in 1947 and is the oldest society of the computing community. Dedicated to the development of information processing as a discipline and to the responsible use of computers, ACM has over 50,000 members. ACM publishes eight major periodicals, offers 32 special interest groups, and recognizes over 400 chapters and student chapters. ACM sponsors a variety of national, regional and local conferences, seminars and programs.
11 West 42nd Street • 3rd Floor • New York, NY 10036

ACPA: The *Association of Computer Programmers and Analysts* is an international organization of professionals dedicated to providing service to its membership, the profession and to the public. ACPA offers its members a voice on professional issues, and opportunities to develop professional skills through seminars, workshops and conferences. ACPA provides informative national and chapter publications, and promotes interchange of ideas with other professionals at chapter activities.
504 North Lincoln Street • Arlington, VA 22201

AEDS: The *Association for Educational Data Systems* is a private, non-profit educational organization founded in 1962. AEDS provides a forum for the exchange of

ideas and information about the relationship of modern technology to modern education. This is accomplished through the three quarterly publications, AEDS BULLETIN, AEDS JOURNAL and AEDS MONITOR; an annual conference; national, regional and local workshops and an annual computer programming contest for secondary school students. AEDS is affiliated with the American Federation of Information Processing Societies (AFIPS), and disseminates information through its own functional and geographic affiliates.
1201 Sixteenth Street, N.W. • *Washington, DC 20036*

AICCP: The *Association of the Institute for Certification of Computer Professionals* is the official certificate holder membership group of the ICCP. There are two classes of membership consisting of active (dues paying) and inactive. The AICCP is directly involved in supporting the ICCP and the interests of the certificate holders.
35 East Wacker Drive • *Chicago, IL 60601*

A1A: The *Automation 1 Association* is dedicated to the professional growth of its members through monthly technical seminars, monthly dinner meetings and monthly field trips to a variety of computer installations. A corollary to the professional growth offered through A1A is the opportunity for lasting friendships with people of similar interests.
7380 Parkway Drive • *La Mesa, CA 92041*

CIPS: The *Canadian Information Processing Society* was formed in 1958 to bring together Canadians with a common interest in the field of information processing. The current membership of over 4,000 persons includes scientists, businessmen and others who make their careers in computing and information processing.
243 College Street, 5th Floor • *Toronto, Ontario, Canada M5T 2Y1*

DPMA: The *Data Processing Management Association* is the largest professional association in the field of computer management with 29,000 regular and 8,000 student members for a total membership of 37,000 plus, in the United States, Canada, and other countries. The purpose of DPMA is to engage in education and research activities focused upon the development of effective programs for the self-improvement of its membership. It seeks to encourage high standards of competence and promotes a professional attitude among its members.

505 Busse Highway • Park Ridge, IL 60068

IEEE: The *Computer Society of the Institute of Electrical and Electronics Engineers*, by charter, definition and action, is the leading professional association in advancing the theory and practice of computer and information processing technology. The Society publishes three Transactions and three magazines and promotes cooperation and interchange of recent and relevant information among its approximately 62,000 members in all parts of the world.

P.O. Box 639 • Silver Spring, MD 20901

If after reading computer books, trade magazines and information from the ICCP, you still think that a career as a software creator might be the goal at the end of your formal education, emphasize the following subjects in high school:

1. All the math courses offered, especially Algebra II and Calculus

2. English and Creative Writing

3. Business courses, especially Bookkeeping, Accounting, Economics

4. Science, especially Physics

5. Computer Math I—programming fundamentals

6. Computer Math II, also called Computer Science. Especially recommended is the Advanced Placement Curriculum as outlined by the College Board. Programming Methodology, Algorithms, Data Structures, and the standard PASCAL programming language are emphasized. Algebra II usually is required as a prerequisite. If you excel in the AP course and pass the three-hour Advanced Placement Computer Science Examination, you might earn college credit for your efforts.

7. Learn one of the word processors that allow typing changes on a CRT before printing. New word processors are available all the time, but here are a few well-known ones:
   WordStar
   The Finalword
   WordPerfect
   XyWrite II-plus
   Volkswriter Deluxe
   MultiMate
   MicrosoftWord
   WORD

8. Learn one of the spreadsheets that have powerful recalculation features which refigure all numbers affected by a change to any related number. Here are some spreadsheets currently on the market:
   VisiCalc
   SuperCalc
   Multiplan
   Lotus 1-2-3

9. Learn one of the database management packages such as:
   dBase III
   SAVVY PC
   SALVO
   KnowledgeMan

10. Typing (computer voice recognition is still rather primitive)

11. Speech

12. Foreign language

Add extracurricular activities for software sales that provide speaking experience; they will look well on your résumé.

1. Debate

2. Run for class office

The College Board publishes an excellent booklet for students headed for college, *Advanced Placement Course Description, Computer Science.* It describes the AP course goals, outlines the course of study, and discusses the Advanced Placement Computer Science

Examination. If you wish to order this pamphlet, ask your high school counselor for the address of your college board regional office or write Program Service Officer (AP), The College Board, 888 Seventh Avenue, New York, NY 10106.

According to Dr. Kennedy of Rice University: "Students who think they want to major in computer science in college should study lots of mathematics and English in high school.

"The problem that we have in computer science is that students think that taking every CS course offered at the high school level is good preparation for a very competitive college program in computer science. Unfortunately, that is not true unless a high school offers an outstanding program which is oriented toward a college-level program in CS.

"A lot of people are learning about computers in the wrong sort of way. Unless you know that your high school has a first-rate program that teaches, for example, the Advanced Placement course in computer science, I would take only computer courses that emphasize familiarity with personal computers, word processing, and things like that. I would spend a lot of time doing well in high school mathematics, learning calculus and algebra."

I asked Dr. Kennedy why calculus is used by colleges as an indicator of ability to major in computer science when many successful systems programmers now in the field have never cracked a calculus book.

"While it is true," he answered, "that some people can be outstanding systems programmers without having had calculus, colleges use calculus as one indicator of ability to deal with abstraction in mathematics. I would venture to say that most highly successful systems programmers would do reasonably well [in calculus] if they had pursued a college career."

H. Ross Perot, founder of Electronic Data Systems Corporation, also wants to see more students studying higher mathematics in high school. Says the computer magnate: "As we enter the Age of Information, Russia has 5 million students studying calculus. In the United States, only 500,000 are studying calculus, giving the Russians a ten-to-one advantage in advanced mathematics." (You will have to help put these odds in *our* favor!)

In addition to math, Professor Kennedy also advises you "to take some creative writing courses, because the skills that are used in writing are quite similar to the ones that you use in programming. The ability to design a well-thought-out paragraph or an organized passage composed of paragraphs is very similar to the ability to design a well-thought-out computer program. Furthermore, nearly half or maybe even more of a good computer programmer's job is documentation. A programmer needs to know how to write—it is very important!"

If you hope to take computer-related courses in college, you should take the time to observe one or two computer science classes at a nearby college. I asked Dr. Kennedy if high school students can get permission to do this at Rice University.

"Yes," he said, "we have had students do that. Classes at the college level are very different from classes taught at the high school level. A student can at least see if he likes one or two of the instructors!

"Rice has an organized program whereby outstanding students who are considering Rice are invited to visit the campus for a couple of days. They go to classes, stay in the colleges, and are shown around the college by an undergraduate."

Before you proceed with your career plans, be sure to read the help-wanted section of a big-city newspaper in the area where you might wish to work. In particular, study the electronic data processing, professional, or engineering technical categories. I also recommend that you read the Position Announcements section at the back of *Computerworld*.

Nothing brings home the importance of computer training quicker than reading an ad such as this:

SYSTEMS PROGRAMMER WANTED:

Excellent opportunity for an individual with 2+ years of experience utilizing MVS, IMS, and CICS. We offer a multi-CPU environment with exceptional potential for advancement into management.

This ad is rather typical and, in fact, very similar to one I recently saw in the Houston *Chronicle*. Do you recognize the initials? Some of them are in this book.

To help you with this type of computerese, use the glossary and index in this book or a computer dictionary like the *Sippl Computer Dictionary and Handbook*, published by Howard W. Sams & Co., Inc., 4300 West 62nd Street, Indianapolis, IN 46268.

CONTENT OF CDP EXAMINATION

Sections

The CDP Examination is composed of the following five sections, each containing 60 questions:

Section 1. Data Processing Equipment
Section 2. Computer Programming and Software
Section 3. Principles of Management
Section 4. Accounting and Quantitative Methods
Section 5. Systems Analysis and Design

Outline of Content and References

The following Outline of Content indicates the content covered in each Section of the CDP Examination. It is presented to give candidates some indication of the scope of the CDP Examination.

An Official Instruction Manual is available for purchase for $7.50 from:

I.C.C.P.
35 East Wacker Drive
Chicago, IL 60601

The Instruction Manual gives more detailed information regarding the test than this Announcement. In addition, a complete list of references is included. While candidates are not expected to be thoroughly familiar with all the material in the references, they should be reasonably knowledgeable in the broad content areas that they cover. (The Instruction Manual is offered free of charge to instructors of review courses.)

Definitions for terminology in the Examination are taken from the American National Standards Institute, 1430 Broadway, New York, New York 10018.

The candidate is expected to have a practical working knowledge in each of the topics listed in the following outline.

Section 1.   Data Processing Equipment

I. Computers
    A. Evolution of EDP
        1. Highlights of data processing development
        2. Need for and use of EDP equipment

    B. Computer Components and Functions
      1. Memory
      2. Arithmetic and logic
      3. Control
      4. Input/Output
    C. Internal Processing
      1. Data representation-code structures
      2. Memory and registers
      3. Channels
      4. Interrupt
      5. Memory protect
      6. Floating point
      7. Microprograms
    D. Computer Characteristics
      1. Commercial, scientific, and process control
      2. Serial, parallel, and vector
      3. Multiprogramming
      4. Virtual memory
      5. Multiprocessing
      6. Data base processors
II. Peripherals
    A. Input/Output Devices and Media
      1. Card readers/punches
      2. Direct access I/O
      3. Paper tape readers/punches
      4. Display terminals
      5. Hard copy terminals
      6. Printers
      7. Consoles
      8. Diskette readers/recorders
      9. Key to tape/disks
    B. Special Input/Output Systems
      1. Magnetic ink character readers
      2. Optical character readers
      3. Com (computer output microfilm)
      4. Voice input/output
      5. Point of origin terminals
      6. Touch tone
      7. Large screen display
    C. Data Transmission
      1. Digital and analog lines
      2. Synchronous and asynchronous transmissions

  3. Switched/leased/proprietary lines
  4. Line grades
  5. Modems and interface devices
  6. Multiplexors and concentrators
  7. Communication controllers
  8. Message protocol
  9. Simplex and duplex transmissions
 D. Auxiliary Memory
  1. Magnetic tape
  2. Disks/drums
  3. Mass storage

References for Section 1

Abrams and Stein, *Computer Hardware and Software*, Addison Wesley, 1975.

Awad, Elias M., *Business Data Processing*, Prentice-Hall, 1980.

Chorafas, Dimitris, *Data Communications for Distributed Information Systems*, Petrocelli Books, 1980.

Dock, V. Thomas and Essick, Edward L., *Principles of Business Data Processing with MIS*, Science Research Associates, 1980.

Hellerman, H., *Digital Computer System Principles*, McGraw-Hill, 1976.

Housley, Trevor, *Data Communications and Teleprocessing Systems*, Prentice-Hall, 1979.

Kroenke, David M., *Business Computer Systems: An Introduction*, Mitchell Publishing, 1981.

Mano, M.M., *Computer System Architecture*, Prentice-Hall, 1976.

Pooch, U. and Chattergy, R., *Minicomputers: Hardware, Software and Selection*, West, 1980.

Stone, Harold, *Introduction to Computer Architecture*, Science Research Associates, 1980.

Thierauf, Robert J., *Distributed Processing Systems,* Prentice-Hall, 1978.

Section 2.   Computer Programming and Software

 I. Principles of Programming
 A. Basic Computer Instructions
  1. Data transfer
  2. Arithmetic
  3. Decision

      4. Input/Output
      5. Special purpose
   B. Methods of Addressing
      1. Direct
      2. Indirect
      3. Registers
   C. Loops
      1. Initialization
      2. Processing
      3. Modification and control
   D. Subroutines
      1. Calling sequences and parameters
      2. Open and closed
      3. Macros
      4. Reenterable and serial reusable
   E. Program Checking
      1. Memory dumps
      2. Dynamic tracing
   F. Basic Programming Techniques
      1. Charts and diagrams
      2. Decision tables
      3. Data editing and error detection
      4. Restart points
      5. Documentation
      6. Run time estimating
   G. Input/Output Considerations
      1. Access methods
      2. Performance characteristics
   H. Structured Techniques
      1. Design
      2. Programming
 II. Meta Programming Systems
   A. Assemblers, compilers
   B. Generators
   C. Operating Systems
   D. Utilities
   E. Data Base Management Systems
III. Programming Languages
   A. Application, Scope, and Usage
      1. Procedure languages
      2. Interactive languages
      3. Simulation languages

    4. Assembly languages
    5. Report program generators
    6. List processing languages
  B. COBOL
    1. Identification division
    2. Environment division
    3. Data division
    4. Procedure division

References for Section 2

Atre, Steve, *Data Base: Structured Techniques for Design, Performance and Management*, John Wiley and Sons, 1980.

Bohl, Marilyn, *Tools for Structured Design*, Science Research Associates, 1978.

Calingaert, Peter, *Assemblers, Compilers and Program Translation*, Computer Sciences, 1979.

Freeman, Peter, *Software Systems Principles*, Science Research Associates, 1975.

Katzan, Harry, *Operating Systems: A Pragmatic Approach*, Van Nostrand Reinhold, 1983.

Kroenke, David, *Database Processing: Fundamentals, Design, Implementation*, Science Research Associates, 1983.

Martin, James, *Computer Database Organization*, Prentice-Hall, 1977.

Shelly, Gary B. and Cashman, Thomas J., *Advanced Structured COBOL*, Anaheim Publishing, 1978.

Weiland, Richard, *The Programmer's Craft*, Reston, 1983.

Yourdon, Edward, *Techniques of Program Structure and Design*, Prentice-Hall, 1975.

Section 3.   Principles of Management

  I. Principles of General Management
    A. Organizational Principles
      1. Senior, functional, and supervisory managers' responsibilities
      2. Line, staff, and service concepts
      3. Centralization and decentralization concepts
    B. Planning Principles
      1. Policy and strategy formulation
      2. Policy and strategy implementation

3. Planning process
4. Decision-making process
C. Control and Direction Principles
   1. Measurement and evaluation of performance
   2. Delegation of authority and responsibility
   3. Leadership styles, morale, and discipline
   4. Auditing and regulation
D. Staffing and Personnel Principles
   1. Individual and group behavior–human relations
   2. Organization change and development
   3. Personnel hiring, training, and career planning
   4. Manager selection, appraisal, and development
II. Principles of Data Processing Management
A. General Data Processing Management
   1. Corporate organization considerations
   2. Data processing organization and administration
   3. Data processing strategic and tactical planning
   4. Contracts and negotiations
B. Project Management
   1. Management and user roles
   2. System development methodology
   3. Planning and scheduling
   4. Team organization
   5. Project controls
   6. Project evaluation
   7. Cost benefit analysis
C. Management of the Operations Process
   1. Computer center operations — centralized and decentralized
   2. Technical services
   3. Hardware and software performance
D. Management of Quality and Continuity
   1. Security — physical and data
   2. Standards — development and operational
   3. Quality assurance and auditing
   4. Contingency planning
   5. Privacy
   6. Ethics

References for Section 3

Alter, Steven L., *Decision Support Systems*, Addison-Wesley, 1980.

Auer, Joseph and Harris, Charles E., *Computer Contract Negotiations*, Van Nostrand Reinhold, 1981.
Bigelow, Robert and Nycum, Susan B., *Your Computer and the Law*, Prentice-Hall, 1975.
Carlisle, Howard, *Management: Concepts, Methods and Applications*, Science Research Associates, 1982.
Freed, Louis, *Practical Data Processing Management*, Reston Publishing, 1979.
McLean, Ephraim R. and Soden, John, *Strategic Planning for MIS*, John Wiley and Sons, 1977.
Mintzberg, Henry, *The Structuring of Organizations*, Prentice-Hall, 1979.
Riley, M. J., *Management Information Systems*, Holden-Day, 1981.
Schaeffer, Howard, *Data Center Operations*, Prentice-Hall, 1981.
Singer, Larry, *The Data Processing Manager's Survival Manual*, Wiley, 1982.

Section 4. Accounting & Quantitative Methods

I. Accounting
   A. The Basic Accounting Process
      1. The accounting equation and period
      2. Cash and accrual concepts
      3. Depreciation and amortization
      4. Effect of transactions
      5. Financial reports
   B. Cost Accounting
      1. Costing methods
      2. Cost classification principles
      3. Variance analysis
      4. Inventory valuation methods
   C. Accounting Applications
      1. Accounts receivable
      2. Accounts payable
      3. General ledger
      4. Payroll
      5. Other accounting
   D. Computer Auditing and Control
      1. The audit process
      2. Segregation of function

3. Processing control
4. Impact of advanced systems
E. Use of Accounting and Financial Information
  1. Financial planning
  2. Financial control
  3. Management reporting
  4. Financial statement analysis
II. Quantitative Methods
  A. Mathematics
    1. Notation and computation
    2. Time series analysis
    3. Graphical analysis
  B. Statistics
    1. Probability theory
    2. Descriptive statistics
    3. Statistical inference
    4. Hypothesis testing
    5. Correlation and regression analysis
  C. Management Science (O.R.)
    1. Deterministic methods
    2. Stochastic methods
    3. Simulation methods
    4. Decision theory
    5. Critical path analysis
    6. Forecasting methods
    7. Queuing theory
  D. Mathematics of Finance and Accounting
    1. Interest calculations
    2. Depreciation calculations
    3. Cost-volume analysis

References for Section 4

Anthony and Welsch, *Management Accounting*, Irwin, 1977.

Berenson, Mark and Levine, David, *Basic Business Statistics: Concepts and Applications*, Prentice-Hall, 1983.

Clark, Frank, *Mathematics for Data Processing*, Reston, 1983.

Davis, Gordon B., Schaller, Carol A., and Adams, Donald L., *Auditing and EDP*, American Institute of Certified Public Accountants, 1981.

Kossack, *Introduction to Statistics and Computer Programming*, Holden-Day, 1975.

Porter, W. Thomas and Perry, William E., *Controls and Auditing*, Kent Publishing, 1981.
Turban, E. and Meredith, J., *Fundamentals of Management Science*, Business Publications, 1981.
Weber, Robert A. G., *EDP Auditing: Conceptual Foundations and Practice*, McGraw-Hill, 1981.
Welsch and Anthony, *Financial Accounting*, Irwin, 1977.

Section 5. Systems

I. Project Definition
   A. Feasibility Study
   B. Project Scope and Objectives
   C. Economic Considerations
II. Analysis
   A. Fact-Finding Techniques
   B. Requirements Definition
   C. Structured Analysis
III. Design
   A. Outputs
   B. File and Data Base Design
   C. Inputs
   D. External Design
   E. Internal Design
IV. Implementation
   A. Application System Software
   B. Conversion Software
   C. System Support
   D. Conversion
   E. Acceptance Test
V. Maintenance of Software
   A. Evaluation
   B. Analysis
   C. Design
   D. Implementation
   E. Release Concept
VI. Post-Implementation Review
   A. System Performance vs. Specifications
   B. Analysis of Operating Costs
   C. Review of Maintenance Activity
   D. Cost Benefit Comparison to Plan

References for Section 5

Aron, J. D., *The Program Development Process: The Programming Team Part II*, Addison-Wesley, 1983.

Biggs, Charles L., Birks, Evan G., and Atkins, William, *Managing the Systems Development Process*, Prentice-Hall, 1980.

Cotterman, Cougar, Enger, Holland (Eds.), *Systems Analysis and Design: A Foundation for the 1980's*, North-Holland, 1982.

DeMarco, Thomas, *Structured Analysis and Systems Specification*, Prentice-Hall, 1979.

Leeson, Marjorie, *Systems Analysis and Design*, Science Research Associates, 1981.

Page-Jones, Meilir, *The Practical Guide to Structured Systems Design*, Yourdon Press, 1980.

Shelly, Gary B. and Cashman, Thomas J., *Business Systems Analysis and Design*, Anaheim Publishing, 1981.

Weinberg, Victor, *Structured Analysis*, Prentice-Hall, 1980.

Yourdon, Edward and Constantine, Larry, *Structured Design*, Prentice-Hall, 1979.

SAMPLE EXAMINATION QUESTIONS

The following questions are samples of the type that may appear on the CDP Examination. The value of these questions is primarily in illustrating format. Correct answers to these questions are indicated on page 81.

Section 1.   Data Processing Equipment

1. In which of the following ways is the digital computer superior to the analog computer?
   1. Speed
   2. Economy
   3. Capacity
   4. Precision
2. Which of the following statements concerning COM (Computer Output Microfilm) is FALSE?
   1. COM devices basically photograph the image on a cathode-ray tube
   2. There are two major types of COM devices: alphanumeric and graphic

3. Graphic COM devices are used primarily as substitutes for impact printers

4. COM devices can write characters at rates up to 500,000 characters per second

3. Which of the following characteristics would most likely apply to a direct-access file utilizing indexes or dictionaries as its addressing technique when processing randomly?
   1. Randomizing formula
   2. Two accesses are required to get each record
   3. Synonyms will be generated which will result in extra accesses
   4. There will be a high incidence of gaps or unassigned physical records within the file

4. Which of the following is *NOT* a significant factor in determining the average access time of a mass storage device?
   1. Character transfer rate
   2. Number of read/write heads
   3. Average instruction execution time
   4. Rotational speed of recording surface

Section 2.   Computer Programming and Software

5. In COBOL, what type of condition is exhibited by the expression: A AND B OR D OR E?
   1. Or
   2. Complex
   3. Compound
   4. Exclusive or

6. A compiler would usually have to produce programs in the form of a relocatable object deck in order to make effective use of which of the following?
   1. Macro instruction
   2. Function subroutines
   3. Floating point operations
   4. Monitor programming control systems

7. In a COBOL program, if the data before editing are 1034, the sending picture clause is S99v99, and the results after editing are $10.34, which of the following is the correct receiving picture clause?
   1. $ x (4)
   2. $99.99
   3. $99v99
   4. $ x (2) .xx

8. Which of the following is necessary to ascertain which program

instructions access or transfer to a particular symbolic tag?
1. Dynamic trace
2. Diagnostic dump
3. Reverse logic listing
4. Cross-reference listing

Section 3. Principles of Management

9. Which of the following is *NOT* an important element in the question of lease vs. purchase of EDP equipment?
   1. Cost of money
   2. Tax considerations
   3. Maintenance expense
   4. Parallel operations cost
10. Which of the following would be considered an advantage in contracting for EDP systems applications work?
    1. Avoids maintaining a permanent staff larger than is required over the long term
    2. Avoids maintaining a large staff of systems programming people and reduces overhead
    3. The organization does not have to take the time to gain knowledge and experience
    4. A contractor acquires know-how about the company which can therefore be used in the future as an alternate source for make vs. buy opportunities
11. The organization chart is a graphic representation of the
    1. power structure.
    2. communications channels.
    3. locus of decision-making.
    4. formal authority structure.
12. While strategic planning is heavily staff-oriented, management control is heavily oriented toward
    1. finances.
    2. planning.
    3. marketing.
    4. operations.

Section 4. Quantitative Methods

13. If $f(x) = X^2 + 5$, $f(5) = ?$
    1. 5
    2. 7

    3. 25

    4. 30

14. With 2 letters or digits followed by 3 digits, how many codes can be created if the letters O, Q, and I are not to be used to avoid errors with 0 and 1?

    1. 66,000

    2. 100,000

    3. 1,089,000

    4. 1,296,000

15. "Burden" in a manufacturing company is representative of

    1. direct costs.

    2. indirect costs.

    3. factory labor costs.

    4. product component costs.

16. To double the reliability of an estimate, which is the same as decreasing the standard error by half, the size of the sampling must be increased

    1. two times.

    2. four times.

    3. eight times.

    4. sixteen times.

Section 5.   Systems

17. The first phase in the evolutionary development of information systems occurs when

    1. management discovers it is losing money.

    2. resources permit the hiring of a system staff.

    3. the decision is made to acquire a computer system.

    4. the growth of an enterprise brings about the need for administrative planning and control.

18. In a real-time control system, each logical message requires 500 milliseconds of control processor time. Each remote control device requires synchronized service 5 times per minute. Which is the best estimate of the largest number of remote control devices that can be served?

    1. 10 thru 19

    2. 20 thru 29

    3. 30 thru 39

    4. 40 thru 49

19. Which of the following is *NOT* normally applicable in establishing the objectives of a systems study?

1. Develop and design the data files
2. Analyze and evaluate present operations
3. Develop recommendations for change as required
4. Review present and future corporate goals and objectives

20. Which of the following is generally *NOT* a consideration in real-time computer systems implementation?
    1. Queues
    2. Interrupts
    3. Priority allocation
    4. Hardware diagnostics

ANSWERS TO SAMPLE QUESTIONS

Section 1.   Data Processing Equipment
1. 4, 2, 3, 3, 3, 2, 4, 3

Section 2.   Computer Programming and Software
5, 3, 6, 4, 7, 2, 8, 4

Section 3.   Principles of Management
9, 4, 10, 1, 11, 1, 4, 12, 4

Section 4.   Quantitative Methods
13, 4, 14, 3, 15, 2, 16, 2

Section 5.   Systems
17, 4, 18, 2, 19, 1, 20, 4

CONTENT OUTLINE OF CCP/EXAMINATION

In the general portion of the examinations (questions dealing with areas I-V), the candidate is expected to possess a reading knowledge of FORTRAN, COBOL, PL/1, and an assembly language. Questions throughout the examinations may be presented in terms of these languages.

The examinations are constructed so that all three specializations (business, scientific, and systems programming) will cover areas I-V of the following outline. Area VI will be covered only on the Business Programming specialization, area VII on the Scientific Programming specialization, and area VIII on the Systems Programming specialization.

All examination questions are consistent with the American National Standards Institute's standards in those areas for which ANSI standards have been published.

Computer Programming—General

All candidates will be tested in the following areas:

Section 1

I. Data and File Organization
   A. Data Formats—Internal and External
      1. Character representation codes (e.g., EBCDIC, ASCII)
      2. Integer/real representation
      3. Field, record (e.g., fixed or variable length)
      4. Conversion (e.g., number, character code)
      5. Packing/unpacking
      6. Parity
   B. Data Structures
      1. Arrays
      2. Stacks, queues
      3. Linked lists
      4. Trees
      5. Record
   C. Database and File Structures
      1. Hierarchical/multilevel
      2. Network
      3. Relational
      4. Direct/inverted/multilist
   D. Storage Media
      1. Physical characteristics of primary and secondary storage (e.g., track, sector, read-write heads, volume, speed, access time, etc.)
      2. Selection considerations
   E. File Access Methods
      1. Sequential
      2. Random
      3. Indexed sequential
      4. Hashing

References for Section 1

Date, C.J., *An Introduction to Database Systems*, (3rd ed.), Addison-Wesley, 1981.

Knuth, D.E., *The Art of Computer Programming, Vol. 1: Fundamental Algorithms*, Addison-Wesley, 1973.

Knuth, D.E., *The Art of Computer Programming, Vol. 3: Sorting and Searching*, Addison-Wesley, 1973.

Lewis, T. G., and B. J. Smith, *Applying Data Structures*. Houghton-Mifflin, 1976.

Matick, R., *Computer Storage Systems and Technology*, Wiley-Interscience, 1977.

Naur, P., *Concise Survey of Computer Methods*, Petrocelli, 1974.

Standish, T. A., *Data Structure Techniques*, Addison-Wesley, 1980.

Tremblay, J. P., and P. G. Sorenson, *Introduction to Data Structures*, McGraw-Hill, 1976.

Wirth, N., *Algorithms + Data Structures = Programs*, Prentice-Hall, 1976.

Wulf, W. A., M. Shaw, P. N. Hilifinger, and L. Flon, *Fundamental Structures of Computer Science*, Addison-Wesley, 1981.

Section 2

II. Principles and Techniques of Programming
   A. Computer Instructions
      1. Data input, output, and file instructions
      2. Data transfer and conversion instructions
      3. Arithmetic operations
      4. Decision and logic instructions: arithmetic/relational/logical
      5. Addressing methods
   B. Program Structures
      1. Data definition
         a. Type definition
         b. Data declaration
         c. Definition of variables (e.g., initialization)
         d. Scope and visibility
         e. Existence (e.g., static, dynamic, automatic)
      2. Control structures
         a. Sequence
         b. Selection (e.g., IF-THEN-ELSE)
         c. Iteration (e.g., DO, DO-WHILE)
      3. Subprograms
         a. Calling routines
         b. Common area
         c. Reentrant
         d. Local/global variables
         e. In-line expansion
         f. Parameter passage

C. Problem-Solving and Design
  1. Process
     a. Problem definition
     b. Identification of constraints
     c. Analysis of problem
     d. Design generation
     e. Analysis of alternative designs
     f. Verification of design
  2. Methods
     a. Data flow analysis
     b. Database design
     c. Recursion
     d. Data abstraction/information hiding
     e. Stepwise refinement
     f. Prototyping
  3. Representation
     a. Data flow
     b. Organization (e.g., structure charts)
     c. Control flow (e.g., pseudo-code, decision tables)
D. Programming Techniques
  1. Order of implementation (e.g., top-down development)
  2. Style
     a. Readability
     b. Ease of maintenance
     c. Ease of use
     d. Ease of testing
  3. Debugging
     a. Error handling
     b. Breakpoints
     c. Traces/snapshots/dumps/profiles
  4. Program efficiency
E. Data and File Handling Techniques
  1. Manipulation of data structures
  2. Summarizing, classifying, selecting, sequencing
  3. Field validation
     a. Check digit calculation
     b. Limit checks
     c. Range checks
     d. Consistency checks
  4. File validation
     a. Hash totals
     b. Batch totals

      c. Check sum
      d. Cross footing
      e. File label checking
   5. File creation, maintenance, reorganization
   6. Sort/merge
   7. Table lookup/search
F. Verification and Validation
   1. Testing
      a. Data preparation
      b. Procedures
   2. Review/inspection/walkthrough
   3. Use of assertions
G. Maintenance
   1. Repair/enhancement/adaptation
   2. Regression testing

References for Section 2

Bentley, J. L., *Writing Efficient Programs*, Prentice-Hall, 1982.

Cougar, J. D., and F. R. McFadden, *Introduction to Computer-Based Information Systems*, John Wiley & Sons, 1975.

Dahl, O. J., E. Dijkstra and C. A. R. Hoare, *Structured Programming*, Academic Press, 1972.

Deutsch, M. S., *Software Verification and Validation Realistic Project Approaches*, Prentice-Hall, 1982.

Freeman, P., and A. I. Wasserman, eds., *Tutorial: Software Design Techniques*, IEEE-CS, 4th edition, 1982.

Glass, R. L., and R. A. Noiseux, *Software Maintenance Guidebook*, Prentice-Hall, 1981.

Glass, R. L., *Software Reliability Guidebook*, Prentice-Hall, 1979.

Kernighan, B. W., and P. J. Plauger, *The Elements of Programming Style*, McGraw-Hill, 2nd edition, 1978.

Knuth, D. E., *The Art of Computer Programming, Vol. 3: Sorting and Searching*, Addison-Wesley, 1973.

Lewis, W. E., *Problem Solving Principles for Programmers: Applied Logic, Psychology, and Grit*, Hayden Press, 1980.

McGowen, C. L., and R. J. Kelly, *Top-Down Structural Programming Techniques*, Petrocelli/Charter, 1975.

Miller, E., and W. E. Howden, eds., *Tutorial: Software Testing and Validation Techniques*, IEEE-CS, 2nd edition, 1981.

Myers, G. J., *The Art of Software Testing*, John Wiley & Sons, 1979.

Myers, G. J., *Composite/Structured Design*, Van Nostrand Reinhold, 1978.

Orilia, L. S., N. Stern and R. Stern, *Business Data Processing Systems*, John Wiley & Sons, 2nd edition, 1977.

Page-Jones, M., *The Practical Guide to Structured Systems Design*, Yourdon Press, 1980.

Parikh, G., ed., *Techniques of Program and System Maintenance*, Ethnotech, 1980.

Peters, L. J., *Software Design: Methods and Techniques*, Yourdon Press, 1981.

Peterson, J. L., *Computer Organization and Assembly Language Programming*, Academic Press, 1978.

Weller, W. J., *Assembly Level Programming for Small Computers*, Lexington, 1975.

Wirth, N., *Systematic Programming: An Introduction*, Prentice-Hall, 1973.

Wulf, W. A., M. Shaw, P. N. Hilfinger, and L. Flon, *Fundamental Structures of Computer Science*, Addison-Wesley, 1981.

Yourdon, E., ed., *Classics in Software Engineering*, Yourdon Press, 1979.

Section 3

III. Interaction with Hardware and Software
    A. Hardware Components
        1. Organization
        2. Configurations
            a. Single processor
            b. Multiple processor
            c. Networks
        3. Physical characteristics
        4. Minicomputers
        5. Microcomputers
        6. Communications equipment
    B. Language Considerations
        1. Assemblers, compilers, interpreters, and generators
        2. Programming, database management, and command languages
        3. Suitability to problem and programming technique
        4. Program linkage and control
            a. Subroutines

   b. Program overlays/segmentation
   c. Linkage editor/collector/allocator
C. Utilities
   1. Memory and file dumps
   2. Sort/merge
   3. File backup/restore
   4. File catalog maintenance
   5. Program library maintenance
   6. Editor
D. Operating System
   1. Input/output processing
   2. File system
   3. Interrupt processing
   4. Task management
   5. Program loader
   6. Memory management
   7. Checkpoint-restart
   8. Processing mode (e.g., batch, demand)
E. Communication and Distributed Processing
F. Computers Embedded in Other Systems (e.g., consumer products)

References for Section 3

Foster, C., *Real-Time Programming-Neglected Topics*, Addison-Wesley, 1981.

Gear, C. W., *Computer Organization and Programming*, McGraw-Hill, 1979.

Kernighan, B. W., and P. J. Plauger, *Software Tools*, Addison-Wesley, 1976.

Kurzban, S. A., et al., *Operating Systems Principles*, Petrocelli, 1975.

Ledgard, H., and M. Marcotty, *The Programming Language Landscape*, Science Research Associates, 1981.

Pratt, T. *Programming Languages: Design and Implementation, Prentice-Hall, 1975.*

Shaw, A. C., *The Logical Design of Operating Systems*, Prentice-Hall, 1974.

Siewiorek, D. P., C. G. Bell, and A. Newell, *Computer Structures: Principles and Examples*, McGraw-Hill, 1981.

Stone, H. S., ed., *Introduction to Computer Architecture*, Science

Research Associates, 1975.

Tanenbaum, A. S., *Computer Networks*, Prentice-Hall, 1981.

Section 4

IV. Interaction with People
   A. Interaction with Users
      1. Problem analysis
      2. Requirement identification
      3. Developing program specifications
      4. Human engineering
   B. Programming Team Relationships
      1. Roles
      2. Structured walkthrough
   C. Project Management
      1. Planning and estimating
      2. Project control
      3. Configuration control
   D. Quality Assurance
      1. Standards
      2. Reviews/audits
      3. Testing
   E. Documentation
      1. System charts
      2. Design representations
      3. Module prologues
      4. Baseline specifications
      5. Error tracking and change control documentation
      6. Test plans and reports
      7. User, operations, and maintenance manuals
      8. Data dictionary
   F. Legal Considerations and Professional Ethics
      1. Privacy
      2. Security
      3. Patents, copyrights, trade secrets
      4. Personnel practices
      5. Contracts (e.g., commercial, employment)
      6. Human impact of computers
      7. ICCP Code of Ethics, Conduct and Good Practice
   G. Professional Development
      1. Industry trends

2. Career paths
3. Continuing education
4. Licensing and certification
5. Professional societies

References for Section 4

Baber, R. L., *Software Reflected: The Socially Responsible Programming of our Computers*, North-Holland, 1982.

Bailey, R. W., *Human Performance Engineering: A Guide for Systems Designers*, Prentice-Hall, 1982.

Bieglow, R., and S. B. Nycum, *Your Computer and the Law*, Prentice Hall, 1975.

Boehm, B. W., *Software Engineering Economics*, Prentice-Hall, 1981.

Brooks, F. P., Jr., *The Mythical Man-Month*, Addison-Wesley, 1974.

Cougar, J. D., and R. A. Zawacki, *Motivating and Managing Computer Personnel*, John Wiley & Sons, 1980.

Curtis, B., *Tutoral: Human Factors in Software Development*, IEEE-CS, 1981.

Freedman, D. P., and G. M. Weinberg, *Handbook of Walkthroughs, Inspections, and Technical Reviews* (3rd ed.), Little, Brown and Co., 1982.

Gildersleeve, T. R., *Successful Data Processing System Analysis*, Prentice-Hall, 1978.

Jensen, R. W., and C. C. Tonies, *Software Engineering*, Prentice-Hall, 1979.

Martin, J., *Design of Man-Computer Dialogues*, Prentice-Hall, 1973.

National Bureau of Standards, *Guidelines for Documentation of Computer Programs*, U. S. Dept. of Commerce, FIPS PUB 38, 1976.

Parker, D. B., *Crime By Computer*, Scribner, 1976.

Perry, W. E., *Effective Methods of EDP Quality Assurance*, QED, 2nd Edition, 1982.

Reifer, D. J., *Tutorial: Software Management*, (2nd ed.), IEEE-CS, 1981.

Semprevivo, P. C., *Teams in Information Systems Development*, Yourdon Press, 1980.

Section 5

V. Associated Techniques
   A. Quantitative
      1. Number systems and conversions
      2. Accuracy and precision
      3. Boolean algebra and symbolic logic
      4. Matrix algebra
      5. Elementary probability and statistics
      6. Random number generation
   B. Systems Analysis
      1. System life cycle
      2. Feasibility analysis
      3. Cost/benefit analysis
      4. Implementation planning
      5. System specification
      6. System design
      7. System prototyping
      8. System testing
      9. Structured techniques

References for Section 5

De Marco, T., *Structured Analysis and System Specification*, Yourdon Press, 1978.
Lipschutz, S., *Schaum's Outline of Discrete Mathematics*, McGraw-Hill, 1976.
Orr, K., *Structured Systems Development*, Yourdon Press, 1977.
Page-Jones, M., *The Practical Guide to Structured Systems Design*, Yourdon Press, 1980.
Stone, H. S., *Discrete Mathematical Structures and Their Applications*, Science Research Associates, 1973.

Computer Programming—Specialization

Candidates will choose one of the following specializations at the time of application:

Section 6

VI. Specialization—Business Programming
   A. Languages
      1. Detailed knowledge of COBOL

2. Conceptual knowledge of RPG
3. Structured programming techniques in COBOL
B. Computer Application Systems
   1. Accounting and auditing
   2. Payroll and personnel
   3. Marketing/sales
   4. Material/inventory
   5. Financial
   6. Production control
   7. Management
   8. Office automation
C. System Controls
   1. Data control
   2. Access control
D. Database
   1. Architecture
   2. Management systems
E. User Interface
   1. Interactive data entry
   2. Interactive data retrieval
   3. Special methods
      a. Computer output microfilm (COM)
      b. Point-of-sale
      c. Word processing
      d. Graphics
      e. End-user languages

References for Section 6

American National Standards Institute, *American National Standard Programming Language COBOL X3.23.*

Anthony, R. N., and G. A. Welsch, *Fundamentals of Management Accounting*, Irwin, 3rd edition, 1981.

Brown, G. D., *Beyond COBOL: Survival in Business Applications Programming*, John Wiley & Sons, 1981.

Date, C. J., *An Introduction to Database Systems*, Addison-Wesley, 3rd edition, 1981.

Diebold Group, ed., *Automatic Data Processing Handbook*, McGraw-Hill, 1977.

Fernandez, E. B., R. C. Summers, and C. Wood, *Database Security and Integrity*, Addison-Wesley, 1981.

Mair, W. C., et al., *Computer Control and Audit*, QED, 1976.

Martin, J., *Application Development Without Programmers*, Prentice-Hall, 1982.

Martin, J., *Strategic Data-Planning Methodologies*, Prentice-Hall, 1982.

Martin, J., *Design and Strategy for Distributed Data Processing*, Prentice-Hall, 1981.

Martin, J., *Design of Man-Computer Dialogues*, Prentice-Hall, 1973.

McCracken, D., *A Simplified Guide to Structured Programming in COBOL*, John Wiley & Sons, 1976.

Myers, S. E., *RPG-II With Business Applications*, Reston, 1979.

Weinberg, G. M., et al., *High Level COBOL Programming*, Winthrop, 1977.

Willoughby, T. C., and J. Senn, *Business Systems, Association for Systems Management*, 1975.

Section 7

VII. Specialization—Scientific Programming
  A. Language
    1. Detailed knowledge of FORTRAN
    2. Structured programming techniques
  B. Fundamental Concepts
    1. Numerical methods
      a. Interpolation/approximation/integration
      b. Systems of equations
      c. Solution of differential equations
      d. Optimization techniques
      e. Error analysis
    2. Statistical methods
      a. Descriptive
      b. Inferential
      c. Probability
    3. Simulation/modeling
    4. Representation, storage, and retrieval of scientific data
    5. Floating point arithmetic
  C. Computer Application Systems
    1. Graphics
    2. Numerical control
    3. Process control
    4. Simulation

5. Optimization
6. Image processing
7. Computer-aided design and manufacturing (CAD/CAM)
D. Hardware/Software Interface
   1. Graphics
   2. Data communications
   3. Analog/digital conversions

References for Section 7

American National Standards Institute, *American National Standard Programming Language Fortran X3.9.*

American National Standards Institute, *American National Standard Graphical Kernel System (GKS) X3H3.*

Castleman, K. R., *Digital Image Processing*, Prentice-Hall, 1979.

Foley, J. and A. van Dam, *Fundamentals of Interactive Computer Graphics*, Addison-Wesley, 1982.

Forsythe, G. E., M. A. Malcolm, and C. B. Moler, *Computer Methods for Mathematical Computations*, Prentice-Hall, 1977.

Gear, C. W., *Numerical Initial Value Problems in Ordinary Differential Equations*, Prentice-Hall, 1971.

Hamming, R. W., *Numerical Methods for Scientists and Engineers*, McGraw-Hill, 1973.

Katzan, H., *Fortran 77*, Van Nostrand-Reinholt, 1978.

Kempthorne, O., and L. Folks, *Probability, Statistics, and Data Analysis*, Iowa State University Press, 1971.

Lewis, T. G., and B. J. Smith, *Computer Principles of Modeling and Simulation*, Houghton-Mifflin, 1979.

McGowen, C. L., and R. J. Kelly, *Top-Down Structured Programming Techniques*, Petrocelli/Charter, 1975.

Meissner, L. P., and E. I. Organick, *Fortran 77: Featuring Structured Programming*, Addison-Wesley, 3rd edition, 1980.

Melsa, J. L., and D. G. Schultz, *Linear Control Systems*, McGraw-Hill, 1976.

Mitchell, A. R., and R. Wait, *The Finite Element Method in Partial Differential Equations*, John Wiley & Sons, 1977.

Newman, W. and R. Sproull, *Principles of Interactive Computer Graphics*, (2nd ed.), McGraw-Hill, 1979.

Pizer, S. M., *Numerical Computing and Mathematical Analysis*, SRA, 1975.

Traub, J. F., *Iterative Techniques for the Solution of Equations*, Chelsea, 2nd edition, 1981.
Zeigler, B. P., *Theory of Modelling and Simulation*, John Wiley & Sons, 1976.

Section 8

VIII. Specialization—Systems Programming
    A. Languages
        1. Assembly language concepts
        2. Reading knowledge of Pascal
    B. Operating Systems
        1. Processor dispatching
        2. Interrupt handling
        3. Paging supervisor
        4. Resource allocation
        5. Input/output spooling
        6. Operator communication
        7. Program loading
        8. Memory protection and privileged instructions
        9. Security
    C. Language Processing
        1. Parsing and syntactic/semantic analysis
        2. Code generation and optimization
        3. Module collection and address resolution
        4. Development techniques
    D. Concurrent and Distributed Processing
        1. Communication protocols
        2. Network architecture
        3. Multi-tasking
        4. Dynamic resource allocation
        5. Fault-tolerance and recovery
        6. Security
    E. Data Management Systems
        1. Physical data structure
        2. Logical data models
        3. Concurrent access control
        4. Data integrity
    F. Computer Architecture and Implementation
    G. Performance Evaluation
        1. Performance measurement
        2. Modeling and simulation

   3. Tuning
H. Software Tools
I. System Management (e.g., software installation and tailoring)

References for Section 8

Aho, A. E., and J. D. Ullman, *Principles of Compiler Design*, Addison-Wesley, 1977.

Anderson, T. and P. A. Lee, *Fault Tolerance Principles and Practice*, Prentice-Hall, 1981.

Brinch-Hansen, P., *The Architecture of Concurrent Programs*, Prentice-Hall, 1977.

Date, C. J., *An Introduction to Database Systems*, Addison-Wesley, 3rd edition, 1981.

Ferrari, D., *Computer System Performance Evaluation*, Prentice-Hall, 1978.

Gear, C. W., *Computer Organization and Programming*, McGraw-Hill, 1979.

Haberman, A. N., *Introduction to Operating System Design*, Science Research Associates, 1976.

Holt, R. C., et al., *Structured Concurrent Programming With Operating System Applications*, Addison-Wesley, 1978.

Hunke, H., ed., *Software Engineering Environments*, North-Holland, 1981.

IEEE, *IEEE Standard Pascal Computer Programming Language*, IEEE, 1982.

Knuth, D. E., *The Art of Computer Programming, Vol. 1: Fundamental Algorithms*, Addison-Wesley, 1973.

Madnick, S. E., and J. J. Donovan, *Operating Systems*, McGraw-Hill, 1974.

McNamara, J. E., *Technical Aspects of Data Communication*, Digital Press, 1977.

Shaw, A. C., *The Logical Design of Operating Systems*, Prentice-Hall, 1974.

Tanenbaum, A. S., *Computer Networks*, Prentice-Hall, 1981.

Tanenbaum, A. S., *Structured Computer Organization*, Prentice-Hall, 1976.

SAMPLE EXAMINATION QUESTIONS

The CCP examinations are intended for senior-level programmers. While no specific education or experience requirements must be met in order to take an examination, candidates who do not have broad experience will find the examinations difficult.

The following questions were taken from previous examinations. While representative, these questions are only a sample. The Content Outline in this Study Guide shows the full range of subject areas. These questions will not appear in future examinations. Similar questions may appear.

Correct answers to these questions are given on page 98.

General Section

1. The disk data area for loading an indexed sequential file is the
    1. overflow area only.
    2. prime data area only.
    3. prime data area or overflow area.
    4. prime data area and overflow area.
2. Each READ from magnetic tape is ended at
    1. a read error.
    2. the end of the reel.
    3. an interrecord gap.
    4. a completely filled buffer.
3. In a structured program, it is most desirable for modules on the same level of hierarchy to refer only to
    1. global variables.
    2. data items in each other.
    3. data items in themselves or their subordinate modules.
    4. data items within themselves or passed to them.
4. In binary arithmetic, subtraction is performed by
    1. adding one number to its complement.
    2. subtracting one number from its complement.
    3. complementing the number to be subtracted and then adding the complement.
    4. complementing the number to be subtracted and then subtracting the complement.
5. Read-Only Memory is usually used to contain and prevent modification to
    1. executable machine-language code.
    2. virtual memory.
    3. data base indices.
    4. proprietary data base information.
6. Programs which are executed in a virtual address space should
    1. be linked at execution time.

    2. use symbolic address reference.
    3. possess a high degree of locality of reference.
    4. be self-modifying to resolve external address references.
7. Modern practice calls for the most effort to be expended on what tasks in a software development project?
    1. Coding and debugging.
    2. Defining, designing, and planning.
    3. Component test and early systems test.
    4. Systems test with all components in hand.
8. Which of the following is used to communicate systems development information to potential vendors?
    1. Feasibility study.
    2. Application study.
    3. Request for proposal.
    4. Systems specification.
9. A team chaired by a systems analyst is to carry out a feasibility study for a new system. Which of the following is the most likely role of the senior programmer in the team?
    1. Writing a report of the team's findings.
    2. Presenting the team's findings to management.
    3. Providing estimates of programming time and run time.
    4. Collecting estimates of the volume of data to be processed by the system.
10. Which of the following program design techniques is *LEAST* compatible with structured programming?
    1. Flowcharting.
    2. Modular design.
    3. Hierarchical function charts.
    4. Routines with one entry point and one exit point.

Specialization—Business Programming

11. In COBOL, RETURN and RELEASE statements have meaning only when
    1. they are controlled by a SORT statement.
    2. they are controlled by an entry in the linkage section.
    3. records are passed to and received from an external sort via the user sort exit.
    4. processing involves subroutines in which data is passed to and received from one subroutine to the next.
12. Which of the following is a method of depreciation?
    1. LIFO

  2. Book value
  3. Cost or market
  4. Sum-of-the-year's digits

Specialization—Scientific Programming

13. Which of the following is *NOT* a way to optimize a model?
    1. Simplex method
    2. Branch and bound
    3. Sensitivity analysis
    4. Quadratic programming
14. In the Fortran arithmetic expression X = A*VALUE**.5+36.,
    If A = 13 and VALUE = 9, then X equals
    1. 7.6637E+03
    2. 75
    3. 76.6373
    4. 94.5

Specialization—Systems Programming

15. Which of the following is used to keep track of instruction
    addresses during a typical assembly process?
    1. Base register
    2. Location counter
    3. Page-table entry
    4. Relocation register
16. Which of the following is the algebraic equivalent of the postfix
    Polish expression, CDEF+/+A+BD↑A**?
    1. (C+D/E+F+A)*(B↑D*A)
    2. (C+D/(E+F)+A)*(B↑D)*A
    3. (C+D)/(E+F)+(A*(B↑D)*A)
    4. ((C+D)/(E+F)+A)*(B↑D)*A

ANSWERS TO SAMPLE QUESTIONS

General Section

1. 2, 3, 4, 4, 3, 5, 1
6. 3, 7, 2, 8, 3, 9, 3, 10, 1

Specialization—Business Programming

11. 1, 12. 4

Specialization—Scientific Programming

13. 3, 14. 2

Specialization—Systems Programming

15. 2, 16. 2

Chapter VI

Higher Education—
A Chance of a Lifetime

The empires of the future are the empires of the mind.

Winston Churchill

Picture Albert Einstein, who died almost thirty years ago, alone for the first time in a room with the Cray X–MP, one of the most powerful supercomputers ever built. Would he need a professor of computer science hovering over his shoulder to help him utilize the machine's tremendous computational abilities?

If Einstein should arise from the grave in the decade of the 1980's, he could absorb the information in the most complex technical computer manuals without much assistance. The same, no doubt, could be said of some of you. Most of us, however, need a formal education to achieve our highest creative potential. And practically speaking, the right post-high school transcript can be the key to many exciting professional opportunities.

No one can predict the state of the computer industry fifteen years into the future. What is known, however, is the theory behind modern computer systems and the way programming languages have been used to put these machines to work. A computer-oriented bachelor's degree can expose you to this knowledge, broadening your intellectual horizons as it prepares you for your software career.

Choosing a major at the undergraduate level is an important decision that often is clouded by emotion and insufficient information. In the relatively new computer-related disciplines, where there is a serious lack of standardization of the majors, the task of evaluating the curricula, to say nothing of the college, is singularly puzzling.

To help clarify the confusion surrounding the bewildering number of majors that prepare students to work with computers, I asked Dr. Kennedy of Rice University to explain some of these college programs.

"Typically," said Dr. Kennedy, "a major in computer science (and this is not true across the board because what each university calls CS is university-specific) has come to mean a discipline that is primarily aimed at producing people who *design* and build computer systems. By computer system, I mean some combination of hardware and software that can be used for a computing purpose. In such a system, I would expect to find some hardware and some systems software such as an operating system, a language processor, or something of that sort.

"Keep in mind that a program in computer engineering (CE) typically would teach hardware in a much deeper way than computer science. Someone majoring in CE from an electrical engineering department would learn some software, with an emphasis on the hardware and the design of the system, including a study of the integrated circuits that go into building such a system.

"The computer science major puts more emphasis on the software but still teaches enough hardware to enable a CS graduate to be able to design an integrated system consisting of both hardware and software. CS graduates are typically hired as systems programmers and designers by computer manufacturers and other companies that wish to have a well-trained systems staff."

As the professor said, college computer science majors differ among institutions; however, most teach an in-depth theoretical understanding of computer systems. Programming concepts are taught, but highly refined skills in many languages are considered of secondary importance. Although college language requirements vary with time and among institutions, the following languages currently are in vogue: PASCAL, PL/1, LISP, APL, and ADA.

According to Dr. Kennedy: "A student who majors in management information systems (MIS), or some such program, typically is more interested in applications pertinent to business and managers with emphasis on the management of large amounts of data, databases, and applications programs that are germane to business and commerce."

Other majors that teach students to use computers in business are: Data Processing and Analysis, Information Systems, Information Science, and Computer Information Systems, to name a few. If you major in Data Processing and Analysis from a school of business, for example, you might study programming languages such as BASIC, FORTRAN, and COBOL along with business courses such as accounting, management, finance, and marketing.

"I would point out," continues Professor Kennedy, "that there are other programs besides CS and MIS that are computer-oriented such as applied mathematics, mathematical sciences, and (as mentioned earlier) computer engineering. The first two majors teach people to do applications programming in the area of mathematics or sometimes in operations research, which is somewhat business-oriented, or in statistics and things of that sort. A degree in mathematical sciences would be appropriate for someone who is interested in writing mathematical applications programs or numerical applications programs and who would like to work for a national laboratory, the weather bureau or the National Center for Atmospheric Research, or some large scientific installation."

I asked Dr. Kennedy what kinds of jobs Rice computer science graduates have found after graduation. It should be no surprise that they are offered some of the most exciting positions.

"First," answered the professor, "I should mention that a large number of Rice computer science graduates go on to graduate school. A second group of our students go to work for computer-oriented companies in Austin [Texas] or in Silicon Valley."

Dr. Kennedy named the following organizations as employers of Rice graduates: Silicon Compilers, Inc., Sun Microsystems, Burroughs Corporation, Hewlett-Packard Corporation, Motorola Inc. (Austin), IBM, Intel Corporation, Texas Instruments, and AT&T Bell Laboratories. (Bell Laboratories may be the most prestigious research institution in the U.S.)

"Some of our graduates," he continued, "also find positions in the aerospace industry doing applications with companies like TRW or in support of NASA with contractors like the McDonnell Douglas Corporation. Others go to work for oil companies such as EXXON, where they work in a systems group. Some are hired by national laboratories like the Los Alamos Scientific Laboratory [the most important weapons development center in the U.S.] or the Lawrence Livermore National Laboratory. [Livermore has one of the world's most impressive computer systems, with three CDC 7600's, four Cray I's, and one Cray XMP.] In general, our CS graduates end up doing system programming or system design."

Dr. Kennedy mentioned another avenue open to Rice scholars. "Some of our graduates go on to business school where they get, for example, a Master of Business Administration [a CS degree followed by an MBA is a dynamite management combination] and undertake careers in areas such as venture capital.

"For those students who want to major in chemistry or physics, computer science is a strong side suit; it will enhance their marketability. A bachelor's degree in physics or chemistry really does not qualify someone to do many things except some kinds of laboratory work; however, a bachelor's in one of these fields along with a number of CS courses would qualify a student for all kinds of computational support roles in laboratories.

"Most people who major in chemistry and physics these days go on to graduate school. For these people, CS is still a good idea because in grad school they will use computers all the time to control laboratory experiments. Knowing a lot of computer science is very helpful at the PhD level; I have known PhDs in chemistry with strong computer science backgrounds who have switched and are doing almost all CS."

At the same time that many students are showing interest in computer-oriented majors, industry is luring many computer science professors away from the classroom with high salaries and fat research budgets. This academic "brain drain" has led to a critical shortage of teachers. The result is that if you want to major in computer science at a competitive college like Rice, or any fine university, you will have to be a top-notch student.

According to Dr. Kennedy: "Computer science is an extremely popular field right now. For example, 40 percent of all of the incoming freshmen at Rice indicated that they wanted either computer science or electrical engineering as their major—that is two hundred out of five hundred students. Unfortunately, we do not have room for that many; we have openings for little more than half that number. This means that one out of every two students who want to major in CS at Rice is not going to be admitted to the major or will be unable to finish the major. To my knowledge, this situation holds true at most colleges.

"Getting into a computer science major is going to be, for most students, like getting accepted to medical school, only at a somewhat lower level. CS is a very competitive major, and students had best pay attention to grades in the key technical courses as freshmen if they really want to be approved for the major.

"Now that does not mean that students who are unable to major in CS will not get an opportunity to work with computers. At a college like Rice, they will be exposed to computers in a wide variety of disciplines such as the mathematical sciences, engineering, and many of the other science professions. They may wish to think about whether they would like to work with computers in some way other than just CS. It is *not* the only field for people who are interested in computers.

"Rice has to limit the number of non-CS majors in computer sciences courses above a certain level because we just do not have the staff except for our majors. We do, however, teach two or three fairly large introductory courses. Students can take a selection of these classes and also some applied programming courses. So even if someone is unable to major in computer science, he will be able to take some computer classes.

"The pressure on computer course enrollments is terrific. The University of Texas has adopted a program, which Rice may have to emulate, of limiting enrollment in the CS major based upon a student's score in five or six key freshmen and sophomore courses such as introductory calculus plus a programming course. These are subjects that every computer science major has to take. A weighted average of grades in such classes can be used as an indicator as to which students are admitted to a CS major. The competition is tough—very tough!

"The pressure on computer science will diminish when it becomes common for most professionals to be able to program. Quite often employers say that they are looking for someone in CS when what they actually want is a competent computer programmer. Sometimes the people who are doing the hiring do not know exactly what they want. Employers are looking for a programmer so they say: 'Let's get a computer science graduate.' That may not be the right person for the job; the position may be best filled by a mathematical scientist or maybe an engineer who knows how to program.

"In fact, I know many Rice graduates who are practicing applications programmers or even systems programmers who never went through our CS program. They completed another major and learned a little computer science on the side and now are doing CS as their primary activity."

A small, distinguished school, Rice may be one of the most competitive universities in Texas, and according to several students, computer science is one of the college's most rigorous majors. As one graduating senior told me: "If a student can just make it through the freshman courses here, the load gets easier. I am not stupid—I did *not* take all freshman courses the first year. Unfortunately, some of our beginning students get discouraged and drop out. I try to encourage them not to give up, to get a tutor and hang in there. It is definitely worth the effort!"

A University of Texas graduating senior offers this point of view:

"I tried to pick a college that would vigorously challenge me and maximize my leadership potential without writing my academic epitaph." A most important consideration!

Microelectronics and Computer Technology Corporation, of Austin, a computer research consortium of eighteen high-tech companies, has considerable praise for the University of Texas and its long-time rival in College Station. Says MCC: "Both the University of Texas at Austin and nearby Texas A&M University are approaching world-class status in their microelectronics and computer technology programs." (The author would be banished from the State if she mentioned one of these institutions and not the other!)

Other schools also have excellent programs that will prepare you for a software career. I asked Dr. Kennedy which colleges, other than his own, in his opinion have the strongest undergraduate programs in computer science. Although he said he was more familiar with the graduate than the undergraduate programs in computer science, he had high praise for the undergraduate curricula at Princeton and Brown Universities among the Ivy League colleges, and the Universities of Texas, Illinois, and North Carolina among the large state schools.

These were not necessarily the schools that he named as having outstanding graduate schools in computer science. In fact, two of the three top graduate schools he mentioned below, Carnegie-Mellon and Stanford Universities, have no undergraduate program in CS.

The following graduate programs in computer science are among Dr. Kennedy's favorites, although he said there may be other excellent schools in the field that are not on his list.

Top Three:
    Stanford University
    Carnegie-Mellon University
    Massachusetts Institute of Technology

Close:
    University of California at Berkeley
    Cornell University
    University of Washington at Seattle
    Yale University
    University of Texas at Austin
    University of Wisconsin at Madison

Good:
    University of North Carolina at Chapel Hill

University of Illinois at Urbana
Brown University
New York University
UCLA
University of Pennsylvania
University of Utah
University of Arizona
Princeton University

Since artificial intelligence (AI) is a much-discussed subfield of computer science these days, I asked Dr. Kennedy which colleges he thought offered the most outstanding graduate programs in AI. (Chapter VII devotes more space to AI than the current number of jobs would indicate: The author confesses that she is intrigued with the subject of machine "intelligence."

According to the professor: "Five of the strongest programs in AI are: Massachusetts Institute of Technology, Stanford University, Carnegie-Mellon University, University of Pennsylvania, Yale University, and University of Texas (in the area of automatic theorem proving). If you wish to consider robotics, New York University has a most interesting program.

"Artificial intelligence is not all there is to computer science. It is a good field, but it is not the only field. I would count it no more than about 25 percent in my weighing of a school's quality.

"The other areas where I would look for strength are first, theory, and in particular algorithms and the theory of programming and of programming-language semantics. And I would look at programming systems, which encompasses compiler construction, programming assistance tools, databases, and graphics.

"And then there is the whole area of computer engineering, which may not count as a part of computer science but may be of interest. CE includes the study of computer architecture, VLSI [very large scale integration], and microelectronics."

If you major in computer science and engineering at Massachusetts Institute of Technology, one of the leading competitive colleges in this field, you will study "algorithms and information structures, the organization of programs and information processing systems, the methods of artificial intelligence, introduction to the description and analysis of linear systems, electronic circuits, linear algebra, modern algebra, computational models," and more.

While completing one such MIT program, students receive academic credit and pay for work assignments in industry. Here are a few of the companies or laboratories listed by the college as part of this cooperative program: Analog Devices, Inc., AVCO–Everett Research Laboratory, Bell Laboratories, Codex Corp., COMSAT Laboratory, C. S. Draper Laboratory, Digital Equipment Corporation, Fairchild Camera & Instrument Corporation, General Electric Company, Hewlett-Packard Co., Honeywell, Inc., IBM Corporation, Lincoln Laboratory, Medtronic, Inc., Motorola, Inc., Naval Surface Weapons Center, Raytheon Company, RCA, Tektronics, Inc., Texas Instruments, Inc., and Xerox Corporation Palo Alto Research Center. It is easy to understand why there is stiff competition for acceptance into this program.

One way to judge any college program is to ask business and scientific leaders in the community for their opinion of the school's graduates. It is important, of course, to gather opinions from more than one company so that you are exposed to several points of view.

On any campus, most students will be delighted to tell you about their college. They will brag about the outstanding research work of their favorite professor, or they will gripe about how the least-liked member of the faculty is more interested in publishing new works than helping the students. Try to talk also with recent computer science or data processing graduates; they will know firsthand how their degrees are welcomed by the "real" world.

An important consideration when choosing your future alma mater is the type of computer hardware as well as the systems and data communications software available to students. The experience you gain in college using various types of equipment will have a definite impact on your résumé after graduation. Many software job offers are hardware-specific. In the business environment, for example, IBM equipment still carries a lot of clout. Digital Equipment Corporation also has a large following, especially with engineers and scientists. So find out exactly what sort of hardware environment the institution offers.

The accessibility of computers and terminals also must be considered. At many colleges students are required to drag themselves out of bed in the wee hours of the night to test their programs. Although not totally unlike the real world, prowling around a computer center at 2 a.m. loses its thrill the second time you do it.

Since a college is judged in academia by its graduate programs, more information is available at that level. An important book that evaluates graduate programs is *The Gourman Report, a Rating of Graduate and Professional Programs in American and International Universities*, 2d ed., 1984, by Dr. Jack Gourman, published by National Education Standards, One Wilshire Building, 624

South Grand Avenue, Los Angeles, CA 90017. Dr. Gourman kindly permitted me to reprint his ranking of fifty-one graduate programs in computer science. This resource also covers many other fields such as: Applied Mathematics, Mathematics, Business Administration (MBA), Economics, and Electrical Engineering.

THE GOURMAN REPORT*
1983-1984

A RATING OF GRADUATE PROGRAMS IN COMPUTER SCIENCE

Fifty-one institutions with scores in the 4.0–5.0 range, in rank order

INSTITUTION	Rank	Score	Curriculum	Faculty Instruction	Faculty Research	Library Resources (Computer Science)
M.I.T.	1	4.94	4.93	4.95	4.94	4.94
Illinois (Urbanal)	2	4.93	4.92	4.93	4.92	4.93
California, Berkeley	3	4.91	4.91	4.92	4.90	4.91
Minnesota (Minneapolis)	4	4.90	4.90	4.90	4.88	4.90
Wisconsin (Madison)	5	4.88	4.88	4.89	4.86	4.88
UCLA	6	4.86	4.86	4.87	4.84	4.86
Columbia	7	4.84	4.84	4.86	4.83	4.84
Harvard	8	4.83	4.82	4.85	4.81	4.83
Pennsylvania	9	4.81	4.81	4.83	4.80	4.81
Stanford	10	4.79	4.79	4.82	4.78	4.76
Michigan (Ann Arbor)	11	4.77	4.77	4.81	4.74	4.75
Carnegie-Mellon	12	4.75	4.76	4.79	4.72	4.73
Purdue (Lafayette)	13	4.73	4.74	4.76	4.70	4.71
Cal Tech	14	4.71	4.72	4.74	4.69	4.70
Yale	15	4.69	4.71	4.72	4.66	4.68
N.Y.U.	16	4.68	4.69	4.70	4.65	4.66
Texas (Austin)	17	4.66	4.67	4.69	4.63	4.64
Cornell	18	4.64	4.65	4.68	4.61	4.63
Northwestern	19	4.63	4.63	4.66	4.60	4.61
Penn State (U. Park)	20	4.60	4.60	4.63	4.58	4.60
Princeton	21	4.58	4.59	4.61	4.56	4.57
Rice	22	4.55	4.55	4.59	4.53	4.54
Washington (Seattle)	23	4.54	4.54	4.58	4.50	4.52
Rensselaer (N.Y.)	24	4.52	4.52	4.56	4.47	4.51
California, San Diego	25	4.48	4.50	4.54	4.43	4.46
Kansas	26	4.46	4.49	4.51	4.40	4.43
SUNY (Buffalo)	27	4.43	4.46	4.48	4.37	4.42
North Carolina (Chapel Hill)	28	4.41	4.44	4.45	4.34	4.39
Iowa (Iowa City)	29	4.37	4.41	4.43	4.30	4.35
Brown	30	4.35	4.39	4.40	4.28	4.33
California, Davis	31	4.33	4.36	4.38	4.25	4.31
Rochester	32	4.31	4.33	4.37	4.23	4.29
Johns Hopkins	33	4.28	4.32	4.35	4.20	4.26

INSTITUTION	Rank	Score	Curriculum	Faculty Instruction	Faculty Research	Library Resources (Computer Science)
Case Western Reserve	34	4.27	4.31	4.33	4.19	4.25
Michigan State	35	4.26	4.30	4.31	4.18	4.23
Polytechnic Inst. (N.Y.)	36	4.24	4.28	4.30	4.16	4.21
Indiana (Bloomington)	37	4.22	4.26	4.26	4.15	4.20
SUNY (Stony Brook)	38	4.20	4.24	4.25	4.13	4.18
Virginia	39	4.19	4.22	4.23	4.12	4.17
Duke	40	4.17	4.20	4.21	4.11	4.16
California, Irvine	41	4.16	4.18	4.19	4.10	4.15
Iowa State (Ames)	42	4.14	4.16	4.17	4.09	4.14
Missouri (Rolla)	43	4.13	4.14	4.16	4.08	4.12
Maryland (College Park)	44	4.11	4.12	4.14	4.07	4.11
Ohio State	45	4.10	4.11	4.12	4.06	4.10
Georgia Tech	46	4.09	4.10	4.10	4.05	4.09
Colorado (Boulder)	47	4.07	4.08	4.08	4.04	4.07
Texas A&M	48	4.06	4.07	4.07	4.03	4.05
Rutgers (New Brunswick)	49	4.04	4.05	4.06	4.02	4.04
Utah	50	4.03	4.04	4.05	4.01	4.03
Houston	51	4.02	4.02	4.03	4.00	4.02

*Courtesy of Dr. Jack Gourman

Criteria Used by Dr. Gourman

An institution will be judged for evaluation upon the basis of the total pattern it presents as an institution of higher education. In addition to schedules for gathering multi-dimensional data on quantitative factors, supplemental reports to evaluate that data will apply to the following criteria:

1. Qualifications, experience, intellectual interests, attainments, and professional productivity of the faculty
2. Standards and quality of instruction (Faculty effectiveness)
3. Faculty research
4. Scholastic work of students
5. Curriculum
6. Records of graduates both in graduate study and in practice
7. Attitude and policy of administration toward all divisions and toward teaching, research and scholarly production
8. Administration areas
9. Administration research
10. Non-departmental levels
11. Library

A resource published by the National Academy Press, *An Assessment of Research-Doctorate Programs in the U.S.: Mathematical and Physical Sciences*, attempts to evaluate doctorate programs. The evaluators considered factors such as the effectiveness of the program in educating research scholars and scientists, the research grants to faculty members from the National Science Foundation and the National Institutes of Health and others, and the number and influence of published articles attributed to the program.

Although not all colleges participated in the study, the faculties listed below received the top eleven ratings: Stanford University, Massachusetts Institute of Technology, Carnegie-Mellon University, University of California–Berkeley, Cornell University, University of Illinois–Urbana/Champaign, University of California–Los Angeles, Yale University, University of Washington, University of Southern California, and University of Texas–Austin. The book can be found at the reference desk of many college libraries. To purchase it, write: National Academy Press, National Academy of Sciences, Attn: National Academy Press Sales, 2101 Constitution Avenue, N.W., Washington, DC 20418.

With a PhD in computer science, you will be qualified to teach at the university level. As a professor your influence on computer science would be felt through your students, research, and publications. According to Hewlett-Packard President John Young: "There is a national shortage of 10 to 20 percent in faculty for such fields as engineering and computer science." Says the Stanford University News Service reporting on Young's comments: "Hewlett-Packard provides $6 million for 50 PhD candidates nationally in the form of loans which are forgiven after three years' teaching. . . . The average salary for Stanford PhD's entering teaching in these fields is less than that of bachelor's degree graduates who accept industrial employment."

If, as a PhD, you chose to do research and development in industry and government, you might work at the cutting edge of computer technology. To quote Microelectronics and Computer Technology Corporation: In R&D you will "expand the capabilities of future generations of computers . . . by eliminating a wide range of technological barriers." Chapters VII and VIII discuss some of these new frontiers.

The trade magazines sometimes carry articles about computer-oriented majors. *Datamation* asked the chairmen of seventy-one universities to judge graduate computer science programs other than their own by strength of subject. The results of this survey put

Cornell and Stanford as strongest in theory, complexity, and algorithms. Sixty percent of the chairmen named the University of Illinois as the strongest in machine organization/hardware, while Stanford was top-ranked in numerical analysis.

Colleges want nonspecialists as well as computer science and data processing students to have the opportunity to work with computers. Some of the large computer manufacturing companies such as IBM and Digital Equipment have supported campus-wide programs to get microprocessors to all students. MIT's Project Athena, for example, is being accomplished through "major grants of equipment, software, service, research funds, and on-campus staff support" by the above companies.

Apple Computer Inc. also has helped provide personal computers to the student body in general. Following is a list of members of the Apple University Consortium:

Boston College
Brigham Young University
Brown University
Carnegie-Mellon University
City University of New York
Columbia University
Cornell University
Dartmouth College
Drexel University
Harvard University
Northwestern University
Princeton University
Reed College
Rice University
Stanford University
University of Chicago
University of Michigan
University of Notre Dame
University of Pennsylvania
University of Rochester
University of Texas–Austin
University of Utah
University of Washington
Yale University

The Association for Computing Machinery, 11 West 42nd Street,

New York, NY 10036, publishes curricula recommendations for undergraduate and graduate programs in computer science and information systems. Suggestions for programs for two-year associate degrees also are available. The following books and reports covering various curricula suggestions are sold by the ACM. College libraries or computer science departments might have some of them.

ACM Curricula Recommendations for the Computer Science; order No. 201831; nonmembers $16.

ACM Curricula Recommendations for Information Systems; order No. 201832; nonmembers $20.

Information Systems Curriculum Recommendations for the 80's: Undergraduate and Graduate Programs; order No. 201830; nonmembers $10.

Recommendations for a Two-Year Associate Degree Career Program in Computer Programming; order No. 201812; nonmembers $10.

Curriculum Recommendations for Graduate Professional Programs in Information Systems; order No. 201720; nonmembers $3.

Another helpful publication for the student in search of the right college is the ACM *Administrative Directory.* According to the ACM: "This directory is a biennial directory of names and addresses of more than 3,200 chairmen and directors of Computer Science departments at universities and colleges in the U.S. and Canada, including degree programs offered and on-site computing equipment." The publication costs $12. for nonmembers. Some college computer science departments also have it.

For general college information, *Peterson's Annual Guide to Undergraduate Study,* published by Peterson's Guides, P.O. Box 2123, Princeton, NJ, lists colleges offering associate and bachelor's degrees in the following computer, math, and business-oriented majors: Data Processing, Computer Engineering, Computer Programming, Computer Science, Information Science, Information Systems, Business Administration, Accounting, Economics, Mathematics, and Computer Technology. Majors in all other fields including the physical sciences are also included.

A fun-to-read book, *A Selective Guide to College 1984-1985* by Edward B. Fiske, is designed to give you a general idea of the social and academic reputation of each of the 275 institutions covered. The Chronicle of Higher Education calls this resource, which was written by the Education Editor of the New York *Times*, "the Michelin Guide to colleges."

Another reference book that is full of helpful information is *Barron's Profiles of American Colleges*, published by Barron's Educational Series, 113 Crossways Park Drive, Woodbury, NY 11797. It ranks colleges as to competitiveness, gives median math and verbal SAT scores, reveals the freshman dropout rate, and much more. Barron's also publishes a *Guide to Two-Year Colleges*. You can find these books in the reference section of most libraries.

Scholarships and other types of financial aid are a prime consideration for many students. Financial assistance is available at colleges through grants, low-interest loans (such as Guaranteed Student Loans), and campus work opportunities. Although many awards are based mainly on financial need, some scholarships are given on the basis of academic performance. Assistance for handicapped students and veterans is also available.

If you are headed toward a master's degree, the Association for Computing Machinery, Inc., P.O. Box 64145, Baltimore, MD 21264, publishes an annual, *The Graduate Assistantships Directory in the Computer Sciences*. It is filled with information about assistantships, fellowships, and other important college-specific data such as faculty size, software and hardware availability, and degrees offered.

Fellowship information is also available free on written request from the National Science Foundation, Forms and Publications, Washington, DC 20550. Ask for the *Graduate Fellowships Announcement*, SE 81-10.

Of interest to those who are considering a degree in computer science followed by an MBA, the annual *Guide to Graduate Management Education*, Graduate Management Admission Council, Educational Testing Service, Princeton, N.J., is worth studying. It gives important information regarding business schools and, of course, a guide to the Graduate Management Admission Test (GMAT).

Another excellent resource, *Peterson's Guide to Engineering, Science, and Computer Jobs*, lists over 1,000 organizations in the high-tech job market. If you know the geographical area in which you want to work, look up the state under the section entitled,

"Starting Locations." There you will find many employers of technical graduates listed. The book alphabetically lists companies that participate in job-related graduate study programs that help employees with tuition expenses. Found in college and public libraries, the book also lists organizations that participate in cooperative education programs and hire sophomores and upper classmen during the summer.

For those who want to work as a COBOL programmer in business or government, the two-year programs leading to an associate degree may be of interest. The quality of education available at such institutions varies drastically, so you will need to research carefully any college under consideration. Specifically, find out what percentage of this and last year's graduating class has found work, exactly where they are employed, what job titles follow their names, and the salary range of each position. A visit with some of the school's graduates would also be helpful. The credits earned toward an associate degree may be transferable to a four-year college.

Says one executive: "A bachelor's degree is not for everyone. Some very bright people with a technical bent would get 'blown away' by freshman English at a four-year college. For them, an associate degree is an alternative, provided they pick a top two-year college. Yes, it is true that English is considered a must for programmers, but there are exceptions. Some technical people who quake at the thought of the verbal part of the SAT exam make terrific programmers. In fact, they are key people to the software industry; progress would grind to a halt without them."

Unfortunately, the community colleges may be training too many people. Warns a Texas economist in a report from Stanford's Institute for Research on Educational Finance and Governance, "The average number of openings between 1978 and 1990 for computer programmers is estimated to be 29,600, many of them at the bachelor's degree level and over, while community colleges alone graduated about 10,000 in 1981–82; 16,600 computer specialists are needed per year, while 27,000 graduated from community colleges."

Continues the report by the Stanford University News Service covering the study by Associate Professor W. Norton Grubb of the Lyndon Baines Johnson School of Public Affairs: "While there is some real future for high-tech vocational education of the kind increasingly offered by community colleges, the danger is that educators, like the rest of the country, may be easily attracted to high growth rates and so jump on the high-technology bandwagon, ignoring the fact that most of the jobs are likely to be in other, less glamorous areas." This study was supported by the National Institute of Education and by the Policy Research Institute of the University of Texas at Austin.

Class rank is extremely important to the associate degree graduate; the higher your class rank, the more likely you are to be welcomed into the workplace. Says one Houston area company president: "We hire COBOL programmers with associate degrees, but we take only the very top graduates. We have a fine department; I would put our programming team up against the best of them."

Texas State Technical Institute in Waco is a state-supported technical-vocational school offering a degree in Computer Science Technology (CST) that teaches students to be computer programmers in twenty-one months. This career-oriented program, which is very different from a CS degree from a four-year college, leads to an Associate of Applied Science degree. Graduates complete 88 quarter hours (60 semester hours) in computer programming. (Senior and junior colleges complete 33 to 36 semester hours, respectively.) No general education courses such as government or history are required. A typical CST graduate writes over 120 programs using at least four languages such as COBOL (thru advanced), ALC, PL/I, RPG II, IMS, IBM OS-JCL.

During an interview with Ron Williams, Instructor of Computer Science, I asked him about the above major in Computer Science Technology.

"This self-paced program is intended to prepare our graduates to be computer programmers," he said. "The only entrance requirement is a high school diploma. For students with weak scores in mathematics and reading, we offer a pretechnical group program to bring these skills up to standard.

"The tuition is $80 per quarter for a full course load. This does not include room and board. We have many students from lower income families who receive federal and state aid.

"As far as our placement service is concerned, the last recession that hit Houston caused slower placement of our graduates in 1983. While all of the members of our graduating class of 1982 were placed, only 85 percent of the class of 1983 had found jobs in the field when these figures were compiled. We also have an Industry Awareness Day at which companies set up booths and interview students in a relaxed atmosphere.

"We have a cooperative training program for students with a three point grade average. J. C. Penney in Dallas and Methodist

Hospital in Houston participate in this on-the-job training program.

"Wages vary depending on location. In Houston, the average salary for an entry-level programmer in 1983 and 1984 was $18,257 and $22,800, respectively. In Austin the average salary for a beginning programmer is $17,284.

If you are unable to get an associate or bachelor's degree and still wish to learn to program computers, you have another alternative: a technical school such as the Control Data Institute. The CDI, which was founded by Control Data Corporation in 1965, specializes in computer career training. It offers a Computer Programming and Operations program with courses in Data Processing Concepts, Business Systems Analysis and Design, Structured FORTRAN, Structured COBOL, ANSI COBOL, Minicomputer Operations, Data Base Management System Environment, and Accounting Fundamentals. According to the institute, to qualify to take this program: "You must have two years of post-high school education or equivalent or related job experience and complete the CDI admissions test with a satisfactory score."

Says Susan Busch of Control Data: "More and more of the students attending our twenty-eight Control Data Institutes nationwide are combining their computer programming education with previous training in other areas and/or with a variety of work experiences. The major advantage of combining skills is easier job placement. Companies are more apt to hire someone who is already familiar with their specific industry than someone who has little or no understanding of their operations."

James Cantrell, director of the Control Data Institute in Burlington, in an article by Desirée French published in the Boston *Globe*, warns you to beware of heavy sales jobs and schools that make promises. "Anyone who promises to find you a job would be lying," says Cantrell. Although all commercial schools are supposed to be licensed by the Education Department, the training available varies considerably.

Can you find a job as a programmer with no education other than a high school diploma? Some self-educated programmers now in the field have no degree beyond high school; however, during this decade an entry-level résumé with no post-high school education will face increasingly tough competition from those with some college computer courses, bachelor's degrees, and other advanced courses of study. If you have exceptional logical or mathematical abilities and are "test-wise," a few companies might offer to train you without an associate or bachelor's degree, but they will not be easy to find. If you possess this type of talent, why not consider higher education? It will not only help get you in the door, it should also improve your upward mobility.

Chapter VII

Artificial Intelligence: Building the Software of the Future?

Knowledge is power, and the computer is an amplifier of that power. Those nations that master the new knowledge technology will have a cultural and political ascendancy.

In Europe it has happened before: with the invention of the Gutenberg printing press and the subsequent rapid spread of European culture and influence. Within a nation, we can envision an ever-widening gap between the knowledge "haves" and "have-nots."

Professor Edward A. Feigenbaum
Stanford Department of Computer Science

"The Fifth Generation: A new breed of supercomputers so fast they can surpass today's machines a thousand times over, so smart that they can outthink humans. Science fiction? Not quite," say artificial intelligence pioneer Dr. Edward A. Feigenbaum and distinguished science writer Pamela McCorduck.

"Japan has proclaimed to the world that in ten years it intends to develop and market the Fifth Generation of Computers—artificially intelligent machines that can reason, draw conclusions, make judgments, and even understand the written and spoken word," says the provocative book *The Fifth Generation: Artificial Intelligence and Japan's Computer Challenge to the World.** "In a crash program, comparable to the U.S. space effort, Japan has gathered the best

*Edward A. Feigenbaum, *The Fifth Generation*, © 1983, Addison-Wesley, Reading, Massachusetts. Pp. 80, 81 (excerpted material). Reprinted with permission.

and the brightest under a charismatic leader and backed the enterprise with substantial resources."

The kind of intense intellectual excitement found only at the frontier of scientific research surrounds the subdiscipline of computer science known as artificial intelligence (AI). Inspired by writers like Isaac Asimov and nourished by Nobel Prize winners and computer scientists, AI is dedicated to the creation of "intelligent" computer systems capable of perceiving, reasoning, and learning from experience.

Undaunted by the enormous task before them, researchers in AI laboratories envision the day when easy-to-use computers will communicate with nonprogrammers entirely in "natural" (English-like) language. Some visionaries even admit to dreams of creating software with "common sense."

Are these impossible goals? The Japanese do not think so, nor do some artificial intelligence scientists in the U.S. Although no one would claim that AI will produce computers that are human (capable of feelings and emotion), some experts predict the "birth" of "intelligent" systems in the future. In fact, many U.S. researchers believe that it is vital to our economy and defense to be the first to build such "thinking" machines.

As yet, computers lack the speed, memory, and software to match their creators' learning ability. Nevertheless, some extremely important practical applications have broken out of the academic AI cocoon into the "real" world of business and government. A type of computer system called an *expert system* has been developed that is capable of solving problems far beyond the realm of conventional data processing. As a future software creator, you will want to be aware of this new technology.

Says the Feigenbaum-McCorduck book: "Expert systems are computer programs performing at the level of human experts in various professional fields." Currently, these advanced programs are being applied to chemistry, medicine, geology, aerospace, manufacturing, financial services, education, and defense.

A subfield of artificial intelligence called *knowledge engineering* has produced expert systems that can identify chemical compounds, diagnose diseases, pinpoint mineral deposits, design very large scale integrated circuits, configure computer systems, and more. Such successes have opened the purse strings of industry to the development of knowledge-based systems, causing severe competition for a new kind of highly educated and, at present, rare specialist: the knowledge engineer.

What does a knowledge engineer do? He works at one of the frontiers of computer science. Simply put, he interviews human experts such as geologists, medical doctors, and even champion chess players and encodes their expertise into a knowledge base. He has been trained to symbolically represent this "learned sixth sense" type of knowledge in a computer.

Once armed with the knowledge base, the expert computer system works tirelessly to solve complex problems requiring a high level of human know-how. The program's recommendations, if put on-line, can be made available nationally. In other words, while the machine's exhausted flesh-and-blood counterparts lie asleep in their beds, or even in their graves, their knowledge remains "on tap" around the clock via the ever-wakeful AI computer system.

According to a leading AI company, Teknowledge Inc., of Palo Alto, California: "Knowledge systems differ from traditional computer programs in a variety of ways. Based on radically different system architectures and programming styles, the most visible departure from standard computer systems is the capability of knowledge systems to interact intelligently with their users.

"The explicit representation of knowledge in a knowledge base permits the building of systems that can assimilate and exploit quantities of knowledge that are orders of magnitude larger than could ever be practically incorporated into standard computer programs.

"In contrast to a 'decision tree' approach, where the entire process must be analytically determined in advance and coded into data structure, a knowledge base normally contains only independent 'packets' of knowledge, each of which can be examined, debugged, updated, or altered separately."

The following excerpts from *The Fifth Generation* show a knowledge engineer at work:

H. Penny Nii is at once a pioneer, a connoisseur, and a purist in the field of knowledge engineering. Nii was trained as a conventional programmer, putting together systems for ordinary computers, with all the finicky plodding that requires. After a few years of that, she understandably grew bored and decided to return to school for graduate study...

[After] some ten years' experience overseeing the construction of a number of precedent-setting expert systems, Nii has a fairly standard way of approaching a new expert and his domain...

First, of course, she must persuade a human expert to agree to

devote the considerable time it will take to have his mind mined . . .
Once Nii has secured the expert's cooperation, she immerses
herself in his field, reading college textbooks, articles, and other
background material, in part to understand what the field is
about and in part to pick up the jargon that pervades every field.
Now she is ready for the first interview.

At the beginning, she asks the expert to describe what he
thinks he does, and she also asks him to think about how he
solves problems . . . She generally prefers problems that will take
humans a few hours to solve, because if a problem takes days to
be solved by a human, it's probably too difficult or ill-defined to
be engineered into an expert program using current AI
techniques . . .

Having collected this initial information, she brings it back to
the other members of the team, the programmers. Though the
programmers do the actual coding, it's up to the knowledge engineer to choose which of several available problem-solving
frameworks—inference procedures—best suits the new domain . . .

[The knowledge engineer's] job is so sensitive, critical, and
painstaking that nearly everybody agrees it must soon be auto-
mated unless AI is to be throttled by its own success.

Says Teknowledge Inc.: "To build a knowledge system, a knowledge engineer works with various sources of knowledge—books,
manuals, documents, and human experts, for example—to develop
a knowledge base. By selecting or programming an appropriate
'inference engine' to reason about the problem, the knowledge engineer creates the knowledge system.

"While knowledge bases are specific to a given problem area,
inference engines are general. As a result, the 'generic' portions of a
knowledge system can be built by specialists and applied repetitively
by knowledge engineers to problems as appropriate, saving time and
money. These generic programs—used by knowledge engineers to
build knowledge systems—are called knowledge engineering tools.

"As the demand for knowledge systems has grown, so has the
need for commercial knowledge-engineering software tools. This
demand has created a burgeoning market for knowledge-
engineering tools and related services, such as the training of novice
knowledge engineers."

At present, knowledge engineers are in short supply and their
wages are high. Says Teknowledge: "While appropriate computing
equipment and some software tools are generally available, the most

difficult aspect of creating an effective in-house knowledge engineering program is likely to be attracting qualified personnel. At the present time, there is a significant shortage of experienced knowledge engineers worldwide...such people command high salaries and attractive compensation packages.... [They] tend to be highly educated—most hold master's or PhD degrees in computer science—and so are quite distinct from typical data processing programmers."

Unfortunately, a crisis in computer science education exists. As with computer science professors in general, persons specializing in the CS subdiscipline of AI are siphoned out of research laboratories by industry. According to a Stanford University News Service report dated May 1, 1984: "Industrial interest in computers and knowledge engineering is so great 'it's on the verge of killing us in academe.' About 200 of the *Fortune* 500 firms have established laboratories and have become 'vacuum cleaners' for talent. Digital Equipment Corporation, for example, has about 135 people working in AI."

PhD's who have been trained at world-renowned AI laboratories such as MIT, Stanford, and Carnegie-Mellon often are offered positions entitling them to a share of company ownership, especially if they have experience in expert systems. Some pioneering AI professors, however, have managed to keep their ties with the university while serving on the boards of knowledge engineering companies.

One outstanding example of a successful commercial expert or knowledge system is a program called PROSPECTOR. Says Teknowledge Inc: "PROSPECTOR has been applied by the U.S. Department of Energy to several practical problems and has recently made its first prediction about the location of a molybdenum ore deposit. Test drilling has confirmed this prediction and indicates a major molybdenum find." With this remarkable accomplishment, PROSPECTOR pinpointed a deposit that had eluded geologists for over half a century.

The growing influence of artificial intelligence will become obvious even to the most dubious upon reading the customer list of Smart Systems Technology of McLean, Vermont. According to SST: "The company has focused on three programs of AI technology transfer, research and development...AI education, on-site consulting and system implementation, and AI software development."

Here is a partial list of organizations that, according to SST, have taken hands-on courses in Artificial Intelligence and LISP programming: Office of Research and Development, Central Intelligence

Agency, Washington, DC; Hughes Aerospace Corporation, Malibu, CA; General Electric Corporation, Schenectady, NY; International Telephone and Telegraph, Shelton, CT; Navy Surface Weapons Center, White Oaks, MD; Lockheed Palo Alto Research Laboratories, Palo Alto, CA; and other "scientists and managers from industry, defense, and intelligence" too numerous to mention here.

The oil companies have shown interest in expert systems. Ruth Milburn of Esso Exploration, Inc., says that she is optimistic about the future of artificial intelligence in the exploration for hydrocarbons.

She notes that the Japanese are committed to AI, but so are some researchers in this country. "In the U.S., a cooperative effort among universities, industry, and government is under way to further the development of expert systems and other forms of AI."

The high-tech consortium called Microelectronics and Computer Technology Corporation (MCC) is part of American industry's response to the Japanese Fifth Generation. A procompetitive partnership that works closely with universities, laboratories, and research organizations, MCC has a mission, and AI research into knowledge-based systems is a part of it.

According to the company, MCC hopes "to achieve superior technology advancements by directing research investment into those areas which hold the greatest promise. MCC research will help the U.S. maintain technical leadership through the advancement of system architectures and related technologies for future generations of computing and information processing systems." MCC is owned by the following microelectronics and computer companies:

Advanced Micro Devices
Allied
BMC Industries
Control Data
Digital Equipment
Eastman Kodak
Gould Inc.
Harris
Honeywell
Lockheed
Martin Marietta Aerospace
Mostek
Motorola
National Semiconductor

NCR
RCA
Rockwell
Sperry

Machine intelligence also may be the brains behind "Star Wars" technology and the autonomous weapons of the future. The Defense Advanced Research Projects Agency (DARPA) is the leading contributor to research in AI. In fact this agency of the Department of Defense is a powerful force behind the advance of computer technology in general. DARPA, for example, helps to fund premier AI research facilities such as the Artificial Intelligence Laboratory of the Massachusetts Institute of Technology.

Industry and the military are not the only organizations pouring funds into AI projects; agencies such as the National Institutes of Health and the National Science Foundation have supported research and development of expert systems. According to *Biotechnology Resources: A Research Directory*, a publication of the U.S. Department of Health and Human Services, sophisticated expert systems have been developed to aid doctors and scientists.

An outstanding example given by the directory is CADUCEUS, a diagnostic program for internal medicine incorporating AI techniques. Development of this expert system is under way at the University of Pittsburgh and is intended to aid physicians in the diagnosis of disease. As of 1983, CADUCEUS could provide diagnostic consultation to doctors on 600 diseases and 4,000 manifestations of disease.

Another computer program designed to help doctors, LOCALIZE, draws from its own vast knowledge base on neuroanatomy. According to the U.S. Department of Health and Human Services, LOCALIZE is intended "to aid physicians in the location of peripheral nervous system lesions that may cause muscle weakness." The program was developed at the University of Pittsburgh School of Medicine. According to the report: "LOCALIZE was developed on the DEC-10 computer of the Stanford University Medical Experimental Computer Resource–Artificial Intelligence in Medicine (SUMEX-AIM) network. The program's ability to explain its decisions makes LOCALIZE a useful teaching aid.... Typing the question, 'Why?' produces an explanation of the computer's reasoning, which is derived from neuroanatomic charts and can be easily verified."

One of the earliest expert systems, DENDRAL, was applied to the field of chemistry. Developed by AI scientist Edward A. Feigenbaum and genetics Nobel laureate Joshua Lederberg, this program is used as a powerful chemist's assistant in interpreting the data from mass spectrography.

Another AI program called MYCIN was designed to diagnose infectious diseases. Resulting from a collaboration of the Stanford computer science department and the medical school, the program stands ready to explain and defend its advice.

If the idea of computer-aided medicine sparks your curiosity, you may wish to read the following advanced computer science books about DENDRAL and MYCIN:

Applications of Artificial Intelligence for Organic Chemistry: The DENDRAL Project; Robert K. Lindsay, B. G. Buchanan, E. A. Feigenbaum, and J. Lederberg.

William Kaufmann, Inc.
Dept. AI 23
95 First Street
Los Altos, CA 94022

Rule-Based Expert Systems: The MYCIN Experiments of the Stanford Heuristic Programming Project; Bruce G. Buchanan and Edward H. Shortliffe.
Addison-Wesley
Reading, MA 01867

Research currently underway in *robotics*, another intriguing sub-field of artificial intelligence, may be of interest to some of you. According to a booklet put out by Carnegie-Mellon University, *The Robotics Institute: A Profile*, "its Robotics Institute was established in 1979, to undertake advanced research and development in seeing, thinking, acting robots and intelligent machine systems, and to facilitate transfer of the technology to U.S. industry.... Robots can extend human capabilities by venturing into environments that are hazardous to humans. Hazardous environments in which robots will work include undersea, space, nuclear reactors, and deep-shaft mines. Institute research is currently addressing the problems of navigation and wheeled and legged locomotion, lightweight manipulators and potential mining applications."

Since robots are also capable of working in factories and doing other jobs that some people want to do, the Institute is studying the "Social Impacts" of robots and "Workers' Reactions to Industrial Robots."

Stanford also has an important robotics laboratory. Says a Stanford University News Service report covering long-term labor forecasts by Russell W. Rumberger and Henry M. Levin of Stanford, "Some evidence suggests that more jobs will be destroyed than created by technological change. A recent study of robotics suggests robots will eliminate 100,000 to 200,000 jobs by 1990, while creating only 32,000 to 64,000 jobs."

Those of you who are fascinated by the idea of programming robots may wish to read a periodical called *Robotics Age*, P.O. Box 358, Peterborough, NH 03458. Another excellent source of information about the industry is the Robotics Institute of America, One SME Drive, P.O. Box 1366, Dearborn, MI 48121.

AI software developers use PASCAL, FORTRAN, PL/1, and a number of special computer languages, such as LISP (a number of dialects) and PROLOG, to build expert systems. There is even a language called FUZZY for reasoning about imprecise concepts. To learn more about LISP and PROLOG, the following technical books are available:

LISP, 2d ed., Patrick Henry Winston and Berthold K. P. Horn

Addison-Wesley

PROLOG Programming for Artificial Intelligence. Dr. Ivan Bratko

Addison-Wesley

There are other subfields of AI besides expert systems and robotics that may interest you. Here is one way to subdivide the field as quoted from *AI Magazine*: Automatic Programming, Cognitive Modeling, Expert Systems, Knowledge Representation, Learning and Knowledge Acquisition, Logic Programming, Natural Language, Planning and Search, Robotics, System Support, Theorem Proving, and Vision.

One way to learn more about this subject is to read *AI Magazine*, published by the American Association for Artificial Intelligence (AAAI), 445 Burgess Drive, Menlo Park, CA 94025. Many of its articles are written by leading researchers and professors. The magazine can be found in the periodical section of some university libraries. Students can join AAAI for $15 and receive the magazine as a benefit of membership. According to AAAI, the magazine reports research in progress, reviews books and articles, announces meetings and conferences, and gives notices of job openings in the field. You can purchase the following technical article from AAAI if you are interested in more detailed information about this complex field: "An Overview of Artificial Intelligence," by Edward A. Feigenbaum.

In the last few years quite a few books have been published on AI. Some of the following are considered advanced books on computer science:

The Fifth Generation: Japan's Computer Challenge to the World. Edward A. Feigenbaum and Pamela McCorduck. Addison-Wesley.

Introduction to Artificial Intelligence. Eugene Charniak and Drew McDermott. Addison-Wesley.

Readings in Medical Artificial Intelligence: The First Decade. William J. Clancey and Edward H. Shortliffe. Addison-Wesley.

Building Expert Systems. Frederick Hayes-Roth, Donald Waterman, and Douglas Lenat, eds. Addison-Wesley.

Artificial Intelligence. E. Rich. McGraw-Hill.

Machines Who Think. Pamela McCorduck. W. H. Freeman and Company.

Computer Power and Human Reason. Joseph Weizenbaum. W. H. Freeman and Company.

Although expert systems are already at work, many scientists believe computers "who" can mimic human learning and common sense are a long way off. Even the optimistic Feigenbaum-McCorduck book says that the plans of the Fifth Generation project "are audacious, some would say to the point of recklessness.... The science upon which these plans are laid lies at the outermost edge (and in some cases, well beyond) what computer science knows at present. The plan is risky; it contains several 'scheduled breakthroughs.' There are major scientific and engineering challenges in every aspect of the work, from artificial intelligence through parallel architectures and distributed functions to VLSI design and fabrication."

I asked Dr. Kennedy at Rice for his predictions concerning the future of AI in the next fifteen years.

"As of now," answered the professor, "I know of not one expert system that actually is depended on by professionals to do a job that they would normally do themselves in spite of the extensive publicity that expert systems have received. I suspect that within the next fifteen years that will change, and that certain expert systems will be used as advisory tools.

"There are well-known expert systems that have been proven to do a good job in certain situations. For example, MYCIN is one of the oldest and most written about expert systems. It is rated as good as a member of a medical school faculty at being able to prescribe antibiotic treatments for infections of the meningitis form. And yet, I do not think that MYCIN is used by any medical school or hospital to assist in selecting antibiotic treatments for meningitis infections. This indicates that people are unwilling, as yet, to trust computerized expert systems for advice of this sort. I suspect, however, that this will change in the next ten years and that expert systems will be used in a number of areas.

"I do not think, however, that the grandiose goals of the artificial intelligence community as expressed in Dr. Edward A. Feigenbaum's book *The Fifth Generation*, where he has expert systems dominating the entire society and its economy, will be realized. I feel that expert systems are very good in certain narrow areas. But there are whole areas of expertise and human activity where expert systems are *not* useful.

"There are not really a whole lot of interesting techniques in an expert system. I mean, it is a table-driven program that is able to reason in certain fairly simple, straightforward ways—which on demand can reconstruct the chain of reasoning that led to a particular conclusion. All of these things are extremely useful, but there really is not much more depth in an expert system.

"Artificial intelligence computers are able to prove theorems that are fairly simple—right now. But deep theorems (requiring creative proofs) seem to be harder for computers to attack in any reasonable fashion. And so there has been the advent of semiautomatic proof systems in which the human and the machine work together in a relationship in which the computer does the straightforward things and the human does the deeper things. That is the sort of paradigm which I expect will take over a lot of things where the work from AI will be applied in a sort of semiautomatic way rather than an automatic way to assist humans in doing certain kinds of tasks.

"I guess," concludes Dr. Kennedy, "that is a reasonable assessment of the kinds of things that I might expect to come from AI in the next ten years."

As a future software builder, you will want to keep abreast of AI's accomplishments. The long-term consequences of artificial intelligence on tomorrow's software jobs are a mind-tingling unknown, but AI scientists have made some profound predictions. According to the Stanford University Press, Feigenbaum says, "Automation of software development will take place in this decade and the 1990s. One of the worst pieces of advice you can give youngsters today is to become a computer programmer."

Rumors of the coming automation of programming have been in the wind for years, yet more programmers have been needed every year. With new software projects coming on stream each hour, many business leaders believe that the total realization of Feigenbaum's prophesy is a long way off. Just how long? In the light of the leapfrog advances of the computer revolution, the answer is: No one knows.

Chapter VIII

Potential Employers

After years of rigorous preparation, you will be ready to put your hard-earned education to work. With a carefully built résumé in hand, you should be qualified to join an innovative team where your computer-oriented skills will be focused on the tough problems that face our world. Ideally, you will find a position with an organization in which you can learn and advance by doing—by contributing and creating.

Regrettably, many of us plow through college without stopping to think about the kinds of companies that might hire us after graduation. What shortsightedness! Before you start studying algorithms, nested "if" statements, and binary mathematics, why not at least take a brief look at the types of organizations that might hire you once your education is complete?

To help you zero in on the software job market, this chapter provides a sampling of some of the companies and government agencies that might offer you a position. Unfortunately, many dynamic companies are not included; to cover them all would make this book read like Standard & Poor's *Register of Corporations, Directors and Executives*.

Once you have your college education behind you, you should have many exciting alternatives to consider. For example, would you be happier working for a huge hardware manufacturer like International Business Machines or Digital Equipment Corporation or for a software house such as Microsoft Corporation? If you decide to create programs for a computer manufacturer, will it be one that specializes in mainframes, minis, microcomputers, or all of the above? Or what about a supercomputer company as an employer?

If you choose a company whose primary emphasis is software (not an equipment manufacturer), will the firm be an independent software organization (ISO) with no allegiance to any hardware source, a service bureau that provides its customers with processing results, or a system integrator, also called a systems house, which bundles software and hardware together to create a complete computer system for its customers?

And you have other interesting options. The types of corporations mentioned above all emphasize computer-related products. You might wish to join a company whose primary business is outside the computer industry. For instance, you could help provide information to an oil company as a member of its in-house data processing department. Or what about a job with the federal, state, or local government? Uncle Sam, for example, is a huge employer of software professionals.

Or maybe you will decide not to become a software builder at all, choosing instead another profession where you will work with computers as an end-user. Says Dr. Kennedy of Rice: "Eventually every professional will be expected to be a competent applications programmer no matter what his field of engineering or science. Computers are integrated into every single technical discipline that I can think of and also into many other fields such as the social sciences that are not particularly technological."

Computers, obviously, are vital to the operation of modern industry and government. For one moment, imagine what would happen if computers "forgot" how to do bookkeeping functions. The economy would come to a screeching halt. You might smile at the thought of no bills and tax notices, but would you like to give up your family paycheck?

You can quickly see why a listing of only the large companies that hire people to keep corporate computers humming would read like a listing of the New York and American Stock Exchanges. In addition to all the computer hardware manufacturers and data processing firms, the following types of organizations are also major employers of software talent: aerospace and automotive manufacturers; banks and stock brokerage houses; insurance and health-related companies; energy and fuel companies; broadcasting and publishing companies; wholesale businesses; government agencies and the military; and many more. Depending on your qualifications, you can pick the industry that interests you, and then look for your "company-home" from there.

The mainframe computer manufacturers, for example, are major employers of software professionals of all kinds. One of these corporations sits at the pinnacle of power over the entire computer industry: the world's largest hardware manufacturer, International Business Machines Corporation. More like an eagle than a hawk, IBM's formidable economic force casts an omnipresent shadow over the entire industry, both in hardware and software. Every other computer company in existence keeps a sharp eye on Big Blue's new product announcements. In fact, some people even make a profession of "IBM-watching." Even the Japanese worry about being IBM-compatible!

There are plenty of reasons for becoming an IBMer. Even if you turn out to be a "short-timer," work experience with Big Blue might loosely be compared to having the Good Housekeeping Seal of Approval stamped on your résumé. Generally, the company has a reputation for putting only topflight people on its team. In fact, the IBM esprit de corps is the envy of the industry. It lives in the gung-ho attitude of the company's management-bound sales force, in the dedication of its programmers developing better ways to control manufacturing processes, and in the support of its world-famous customer service personnel. Even ex-IBMers, some of whom say that IBM is short for "I've Been Moved," stand a little straighter when they mention that they were once a member of the team.

Some of you might wish to become part of the IBM sales force. If you are successful in meeting your annual sales quota, the company will admit you to membership in its Hundred Percent Club and present you with the coveted club pin. And if you are one of the *very* top salesmen in your division, Big Blue has a special honor for you: membership in the IBM Golden Circle. This award is cherished by ex-IBMers long after they have left "the business," as it is referred to by insiders.

Many of Big Blue's former salesmen are now top-level executives with other computer companies. In fact, if you look closely at the lapels of the managers of high-tech America, you might see an IBM Golden Circle or Hundred Percent Club pin shining back at you. The point is that IBM has a lifetime influence on its former employees as well as on the computer industry in general.

The following true story illustrates IBM's impact on its people: Many years ago one of its more enthusiastic salesmen brought home a black-and-white picture of IBM's founder, Thomas J. Watson, Sr., for his wife to hang above the sofa. The wife snickered and noted that it did not fit in with the decor. To her amazement, the salesman's face grew red with anger as he said: "This is the picture of the former president of the greatest company on earth! Don't ever make fun of it." Speechless, his wife quietly put the picture in the closet.

Eventually the salesman left IBM to start his own software business, successfully following many of Big Blue's sales and management techniques. Sixteen years passed and the new company flourished, but the picture of IBM's founder was never hung in the man's living room. If, however, you visit his office today, you will see Mr. Watson's newly reframed picture hanging over his executive secretary's desk.

Few companies offer better training programs than IBM: The top software designers attend the IBM Systems Research Institute, the hardware salesmen receive extensive classroom and on-the-job instruction, and the managers are taught IBM's effective management techniques.

IBM has a Tuition Refund Program, which according to the company "reimburses employees completely for courses taken off company time related to job responsibilities or career development." The Graduate Work Study Program "reimburses for courses at the master's degree or doctorate level" in several specialties, of which information science is one. The company also has a Resident Study Program, "which sponsors full-time study on campus in areas relevant to the business, with expenses and salary paid by IBM."

To help reduce its bureaucracy, IBM is divided into Independent Business Units operating in the U.S. and abroad. The nine IBUs in this country are:

> Academic Information Systems
> Engineering Systems Products
> Financial Services
> General Products
> IBM Information Services
> IBM Instruments, Inc.
> Low-End Storage
> Science Research Associates, Inc.
> Manufacturing Systems Products

A trusted friend of the commercial DP manager, IBM dominates the general-purpose mainframe market. And Big Blue's famous operating systems tell these powerful computers "what to do and when to do it." The importance of this systems software cannot be overemphasized. IBM's operating systems have facilitated the great

IBM S/360-S/370 mainframe success story. Why? Because the company's systems programs allow a customer to move his expensive applications software from one central processing unit (CPU) to another without rewriting the code. This concept of upward compatibility has been a key contributing factor to the company's rise to power. In fact, knowledge of a specific IBM mainframe operating system will greatly enhance your résumé, especially in the commercial environment.

In the past, applications software has not been IBM's strongest suit. A team of a few brilliant, independent programmer/entrepreneurs have been known to outperform a whole horde of IBM applications programmers. Since IBM obviously has been unable to satisfy the enormous demand for applications software, hundreds of independent software companies have successfully competed in this area. Big Blue, however, is working hard to gain a larger share of this market.

And what plans does IBM have in the area of data communications? The company hopes to win the race to wrap the globe with networks of communicating computers. Using telephone lines, satellites, fiber optics, and its systems network architecture (SNA), IBM expects to link intelligent terminals, desk-top mainframes, and personal computers to huge databases driven by powerful mainframes. To achieve its data communications goals, IBM will need more telecommunications personnel, database specialists, and encryption experts.

Says the company: "Our programmers participate in the development of information systems—that is, the creation of applications for IBM's own installed data networks ... [programmers] are working in areas of data security and self-diagnosis in the event of failure ... [And] they are focusing more and more on automatic programming techniques, which may enable lay people to instruct the computer in their own words."

IBM also employs programmers in the field of avionics. Says the company: "We are involved ..., with the Space Shuttle, with ground control stations that monitor the flight of commercial aircraft, with interpreting data from earth resources technology satellites, and with sonar signal interpretation."

IBM is, of course, an equal opportunity employer and "has moved aggressively to assure that women and minority group members, as well as handicapped individuals and Vietnam-era veterans, not only have equal access to employment but also get equal consideration for advancement."

Arriving late on the home computer scene, IBM quickly became the de facto standard for the microcomputer industry as many micro manufacturers fell in line by building IBM-compatible hardware—machines that could run programs written for the IBM Personal Computer. Not every manufacturer chose to be compatible with Big Blue; Apple Computer is one notable exception.

If you are driven by the desire to do research and development, you might build your future at the IBM Thomas J. Watson Research Center at Yorktown Heights, New York. The IBM Research Division also has laboratories at San Jose, California, and Zurich, Switzerland. IBM is a big-time spender in this area; its "five-year investment in R&D and engineering hit $13.4 billion in 1983." Smaller companies and foreign countries are hard pressed to keep up with Big Blue's forward thrusting investment in technology.

Says IBM: "The technologies that will emerge in the years ahead—from fundamental research in such areas as lasers, magnetic bubbles, and the fast-switching Josephson junction—will help transform our world.... To help bring about that future, we need engi-

COURTESY NASA

Mission Control Center. In the monitor, the Nestar VI satellite is seen in the cargo bay just after opening of the payload bay doors of the orbiting Space Shuttle Challenger.

neers and scientists in all disciplines. We need both applications and development programmers. We need self-motivated individuals with inquiring minds."

IBM is not without competition for control over the data communications industry. Divested of its Bell Telephone operating companies, the new AT&T is seeking to use its enormous resources to conquer this market. Whether the company will be able to match IBM at this high-stakes game will depend to a large extent on Baby Bell's ability to become known as a responsive problem solver throughout the data processing industry. To achieve its new image, the company will need dynamic salespersons as well as dedicated software developers and customer service representatives.

Among the many other giant companies that should continue seeking data communications specialists are GTE Corporation (Telenet network), Tymshare, Inc. (Tymnet), Control Data Corporation (Cybernet), Xerox Corporation (Ethernet), ITT Corporation, ADP Network Services, and RCA Global Communications, to name just a few.

And then there were the Seven Dwarfs! But only five remain, and these are billion-dollar mainframe manufacturers that are "dwarfed" by the mighty IBM. The seven original dwarfs were Burroughs Corporation, Sperry Univac Corporation (now Sperry Corporation), NCR Corporation, Control Data Corporation, Honeywell Inc., RCA Corporation, and General Electric Company. GE and RCA have left the mainframe manufacturing ranks. The lingering dwarfs or the B.U.N.C.H., as they are sometimes called, continue their struggle to compete against IBM and the Japanese.

With annual revenues of over $4 billion, Control Data Corporation is a leading manufacturer of supercomputers and peripheral equipment. The company has a giant share of the computer services and education markets and is a leader in the consulting business. It also provides specialized systems for aerospace and defense applications.

To serve its data services customers, CDC has established worldwide data communications networks. Its Cybernet teleprocessing network offers scientific and engineering programs that are listed in the *Cybernet Services Software Directory*. This large library covers a broad range of applications, from computer-aided engineering to mining. Control Data also offers time-sharing services to its business customers, including a "full line of computerized bookkeeping and other financial services."

Some of you eventually may go to work for this huge company, which is headquartered in Minneapolis, Minnesota. According to CDC: "Graduates with degrees in computer science or math will discover a wide range of career opportunities in software development at Control Data. These include: applications, analysis, design, implementation, integration, testing and support.... Graduates with degrees in electrical engineering (plus digital training) or computer engineering can utilize their talents in design and development, test engineering, production engineering, and diagnostic engineering."

With over 94,000 employees worldwide, Honeywell Inc. might recruit you to develop and implement advanced-technology systems, especially if you become a computer scientist or an engineer. Headquartered in Minneapolis, this mainframe manufacturer produces a broad range of products for information processing and serves the energy, aerospace, and defense industries.

The Sperry Corporation, which is headquartered in Blue Bell, Pennsylvania, produces large-scale computer systems as well as minicomputers. Sperry's Computer Systems division in Roseville, Minnesota, builds mainframe computer systems and is in the data processing business. Sperry also may hire you if you become a computer scientist, an electronics or software engineer, or a mathematician.

Mainframers NCR Corporation and Burroughs Corporation are two other large-capitalization companies that hire a broad range of software professionals. NCR targets its business computer systems toward the retail sales and financial markets. Burroughs, which acquired the disk drive company Memorex Corporation, ranks third in information processing revenues and is well known in the health care, finance, and marketing industries.

A few of you might be given the opportunity to take on another type of challenge: to write software for the manufacturers of the supercomputers, the most powerful computers in the world. Companies like Cray Research, Amdahl Corporation (Fujitsu controls 49.5 percent of its stock), Control Data Corporation, and Hitachi Ltd. of Japan build the huge scientific computer systems that are used for weather forecasting, seismic analysis, aerospace design, electrical engineering, and biomedical, petroleum, and nuclear research.

Cray Research, which is headquartered in Minneapolis, is a leading developer and manufacturer of supercomputer technology. Molded by the genius of former CDC scientist Seymour R. Cray, Cray Research produces large-scale scientific numbers-crunchers for the nation's national laboratories and colleges as well as for large industrial users.

How much change does an organization need in its hip pocket to join the elite group of owners of computers capable of executing calculations measured in the millions of floating point operations per second (FLOPS)? In 1983 a company with in excess of $10 million could become the proud owner of one of the most superscale processors on earth—the top-of-the-line CRAY X-MP.

Imagine developing the software for machines of such unsurpassed capabilities. In 1983 Cray released a major new version of the Cray Operating System (COS) and selected UNIX as the Cray-supported operating system for the CRAY-2. Says the company: "The new version of COS was critical to the successful installation of the CRAY X-MP because it effectively supports the new architectural features of that system."

Although a relatively small company in size, Cray's impact on science is immeasurable. Spending a greater percentage of its revenue on research and development than any other corporation in the U.S., Cray represents an exciting employment opportunity for a few of the nation's top software builders.

Says the company: "Cray's growing staff of programmers and systems analysts concentrate their efforts on devising new tools and enhancing existing software packages for use by customers.... Because Cray professionals work in small groups with flexible team arrangements, the chances for gaining valuable feedback and making individual contributions are immense. As a recent graduate and newcomer to the staff, you might be asked to help enhance Cray's FORTRAN compiler or develop a new element of the operating system software."

In the meantime, science waits to see what new superscale system Seymour Cray and his staff develop next; the company says it might be implemented in gallium arsenide technology.

Another niche in the computer market may interest a few of you. With the arrival of network-oriented applications came the need for computer systems that could promise almost no "down-time." To fill this demand for computers that always are available for use, the founders of Tandem Computers Incorporated developed the software and hardware for Tandem's NonStop system, a modular computer system based on two or more microprocessors, controllers, and other equipment. The development and implementation of this type of extremely complex software might be rewarding to some of you.

And then there are the minicomputer manufacturers. Digital Equipment Corporation, the world's largest builder of minis, is the second-largest manufacturer of computers, peripheral equipment, and related software. Other important forces in this market are Data General Corporation, Datapoint Corporation, Hewlett-Packard Company, and Wang Laboratories, Inc. All of these companies along with Prime Computer also build superminicomputers, which are built around a 32-bit-per-word processor. As with all types of computers, software is crucial to the support of both the mini- and superminicomputer industry. Some of the minicomputer companies also build microcomputers.

Digital (DEC) was founded in 1957 by three MIT engineers on a concept that as the company states: "... was not only original, it was radical." DEC made computers that interacted with the user and were "small and easy enough for almost everyone to use." Thus, a new product was born—the minicomputer. First called a Programmed Data Processor (PDP-1), the PDP-8 made DEC a billion-dollar company and a dominant force in the scientific, technical, and educational markets.

Digital's president, Kenneth H. Olsen, tells this story about early interactive computing: "The advantages of an interactive computer were never more apparent than at MIT itself, when we gave them one of our very first computers. It was in a room on the second floor above an IBM machine. The contrast was quite interesting. On the floor where the IBM machine was installed, there were two layers of glass in front of this very imposing machine. People entered their problem on a batch of IBM cards. The next day they got their answer back, and it usually said you made a mistake.

"On the floor above, the students could use the interactive machines any hour of the day or night, for any reason, and they could sign up for it months ahead. The reaction was quite different. If you walked in there at three o'clock in the morning, the kids were doing what they do today with personal computers. They were all involved. These computers were so captivating that a number of times the administration thought of getting rid of them because people stopped washing, stopped eating, stopped their social life and, of course, stopped studying. But out of that group of bright students came so many of the things which we take for granted today, including timesharing and even video games. Many of the key people in the industry today came out of that group, and many of the things that we know about computers were formulated during that period."

OPPORTUNITIES AVAILABLE WITH
ONE LARGE COMPUTER MANUFACTURER

Hardware/Software Positions Degree	Electrical Engineering	Computer Engineering	Computer Science	Mechanical Engineering	Chemical Eng./Chem.	Technical Writing	Industrial Engineering	Physics
Software Engineer	•	•	•					
CAD Software Engineer	•	•	•	•				
Hardware System Engineer	•	•						
Firmware Engineer	•		•					
Diagnostic Engineer	•	•	•					
Microprogrammer	•		•					
Software Specialist			•					
CBI Technologist			•					
Mechanical Design Engineer				•				
Circuit Design Engineer	•	•	•					
System & Logic Engineer	•		•					
Systems Performance Analyst	•	•	•					
Device Development Engineer	•	•						•
Test/Software Engineer	•	•	•					
Technical Writers	•	•	•			•		
Manufacturing Positions								
Manufacturing Engineer	•	•	•	•	•		•	
Component Engineer	•	•						
Robotics Engineer	•	•			•			
Process Engineer	•	•				•		
Quality Engineer	•							
Test Equipment Engineer	•							
Semiconductor Product Engineer	•	•						
Software Development Engineer	•	•	•					
CAD Software Engineer	•	•	•					
Programmer Analyst	•	•	•					

Like many corporations, DEC reimburses tuition fees for "approved, career-related undergraduate and graduate college courses if satisfactory grades are attained."

One of the microcomputer manufacturers also might need your skills once your training is complete. As mentioned earlier, IBM is the dominant force in this market. Although a shakeout is occurring in the industry, at present everybody and his brother has an IBM PC-compatible microprocessor for sale. Even AT&T and Zenith offer IBM-lookalike models.

Some PCs are portable. This book, for example, was written with the aid of a computer that generally uses the same software as the IBM Personal Computer. Called the Eagle PC Spirit XL, this "portable friend" has never "forgotten" a page of saved text. Compaq Computer Corporation also is a well-known builder of portable IBM PC-compatible micros.

Some manufacturers of microprocessors have refused to produce IBM-compatible machines. At this time, Apple Computer, Inc. and Commodore International Ltd. are important examples; each has a huge library of programs that will not run on the IBM PC.

As a future developer of high-performance software, you need to be aware of the above-mentioned hardware size categories. Keep in mind, however, that as the mainframes decrease in physical size so that they fit on a desk (some already do) and as the micros gain more memory and speed and are given other mainframe characteristics, these classifications will continue to grow less distinct each year.

The chip makers also are looking for programmer analysts, computer scientists, and computer, electrical, and electronics engineers. Intel Corporation, headquartered in Santa Clara, California, is the world's largest manufacturer of metal oxide semiconductor (MOS) integrated circuits. Now employing 20,000 people, Intel created the first microprocessor. This well-run company is working toward increased miniaturization in microelectronics to create devices with greater densities that allow further preprogramming.

Other major manufacturers of integrated circuits and microprocessor based systems are Motorola Inc., headquartered in Schaumburg, Illinois, and National Semiconductor Corporation, one of the founding companies of Silicon Valley. Advanced Micro Devices and Texas Instruments also are major players in this market. All of these prominent chip makers hire from the entire range of technical personnel.

And there are still further employment opportunities. You may

IBM PCjr, the lowest-priced computer in the company's history.

wish to work for one of the independent software organizations or software houses, as they are sometimes called. ISOs, which can have a work force of one or one thousand, are in the business of developing computer programs but do not manufacture or sell computers or peripherals. Many programmers prefer to work for this type of company whose primary business is producing software rather than for an in-house data processing department of a company whose major business is in another field.

The ISOs specialize in a number of different ways. For example, some are expert at writing programs for mainframes, others build software for mini- or microcomputers, and a few create programs for all types of hardware. Some ISOs build primarily systems software while others emphasize applications programs. Such products can be custom-made for individual companies, packaged, or both. They can cross industry lines or be targeted toward a specific field such as banking, insurance, or health care.

Of the independent software organizations with products for the mainframe market, some are well-known systems software specialists. A few of the companies that compete in this market are Cullinane Database Systems, Inc., Cincom Systems, Inc., Applied Data Research, Inc., and Software AG. For a complete listing, see International Computer Programs, Inc.'s *Data Processing Management Directory*. Computer libraries of some software companies or large in-house DP installations have this resource on their shelves.

Other ISOs emphasize mainframe applications software. Management Science America (MSA), for example, was one of the founders of this part of the industry. The company licenses its applications software packages to banks, insurance companies, members of the health care industry, manufacturers, and government agencies. Known for its payroll programs, MSA also offers general ledger and accounts receivable packages, as well as software for human resource management.

Then there are the ISOs that specialize in mini/micro applications and systems software. They provide custom and packaged software to various end-users. Listed below are a few independent software organizations that offer packages for microcomputers. You probably will recognize some of these products.

Microsoft Corp.
10700 Northup Way
Bellevue, WA 98004
MS-DOS (operating system for microprocessors);
also MULTIPLAN

Digital Research, Inc.
160 Central Avenue
Pacific Grove, CA 93950
CP/M (operating system for microprocessors);
also OWLCAT
60-Hour SAT

Ashton-Tate
9929 West Jefferson Boulevard
Culver City, CA 90230
dBASE III (database for microcomputers); also, FRAME-WORK (integrated software)

Peachtree Software, Inc.
(subsidiary of MSA)
3445 Peachtree Road NE
Atlanta, GA 30326
PEACH TEXT 5000 (word processor, thesaurus, spelling proof-reader, electronic spreadsheet and list manager)

VisiCorp Personal Software
2895 Zanker Road
San Jose, CA 95134
VISICALC (spreadsheet)

MicroPro
33 San Pablo Avenue
San Rafael, CA 94903
WORDSTAR (word processor)

Lotus Development Corp.
161 First Street
Cambridge, MA 02142
LOTUS 1-2-3; also SYMPHONY (integrated software)

A whole other group of potential employers of software specialists are in the computer service bureau business. These companies sell computer services to their customers using proprietary software and either owned or leased computers. A service bureau generally processes input data and returns the finished printed reports to its customers. This is known as *batch processing.* Up-to-date companies also provide on-line services with instant update to files offering customers access to information via on-site terminals.

Some computer service companies offer *facilities management* in which their employees take over and run a customer's data processing installation. Many service bureaus target all or part of their resources toward a specific industry, selling their expertise, for example, to stock brokerage houses, banks, car dealers, or hospitals. Others offer a product that crosses industry lines.

There are hundreds of batch and time-sharing service bureaus, many of which are quite small. Rising communications costs and decreasing hardware prices are causing some service bureau customers to purchase their own in-house computer systems. This has cut into the service bureau customer-base in general and their small-sized customers in particular. The following companies are actively engaged in this business: Control Data Corporation, Electronic Data Systems Corporation (now owned by GM), General Electric Information Services Company, Planning Research Corporation, Shared Medical Systems Corporation, Universal Computer Services, Inc., and Automatic Data Processing, Inc. IBM has reentered this market, and the big banks have been there for some time.

Some of you may choose instead to go into *management information consulting.* If you build an impressive educational background in information technology and business, firms such as Control Data Corporation and Arthur Andersen & Co. may want to recruit you to advise their clientele.

The accounting firm of Arthur Andersen & Co., which has the

largest consulting practice in the world, will hire you right out of college or graduate school and put you through its comprehensive training program—if you have the right college transcript.

According to Andersen: "The first two to three years of your career, you will develop skills in problem analysis and learn to apply advanced methodology to business information needs." As your technical skills grow, you will "expand your knowledge of modern business information concepts—on-line systems, database/data communications systems, decision-support systems, distributed data processing, office automation, and others." The company currently has a consulting staff of over 5,000 professionals worldwide.

Some of you may contribute to another dynamic field by creating turnkey computer systems for the factory and even the laboratory of the future. Software builders and marketers are developing and selling the revolutionary *computer-integrated manufacturing technology* (CIM), which is divided into computer-aided design (CAD) and computer-aided manufacturing (CAM).

CAD software is to a designer what a word processor is to a writer: once an engineer, architect, or even a chemist uses an interactive CAD-type system, he is "hooked"—permanently. From that point on, he will be "unable" to design without his computer graphics terminal.

With the aid of high-powered CAD programs, a draftsman can model products using three-dimensional geometric forms or an electronic pen. He can rotate and analyze the structure of his figure right on the screen. Since the CAD software is linked to a database, a mechanical, electronic, or civil engineer is able instantly to bring up on his sophisticated graphics terminal any earlier designed drawing. He then can modify it, print a hard copy of it, and store the new version back out on the database.

CAD data sometimes serves as input to computer-aided manufacturing software, which facilitates the automation of the factory process by scheduling production, monitoring the inventory, and providing instructions to industrial robots.

Applications of computer graphics software have reached beyond the factory to the laboratory. Through the use of highly sophisticated programs, research chemists can use on-screen, 3-D molecular modeling to design tomorrow's effective drugs.

All of this complex Buck Rogers technology takes person-centuries (200 men working for one year equals two person-centuries) to create. Such interactive computer graphics systems are used, for example, in the design and development of automobiles and airplanes as well as for integrated circuits, architectual drawings, maps, and apparel.

Considering the huge untapped market for CAD/CAM software, companies in this field should continue to pursue software engineers, analysts, and programmers to build operating systems, system tools and utilities, as well as graphics, database, and communications systems. Currently, FORTRAN is the most popular programming language for solving engineering problems, although BASIC, PASCAL, PL/1, and NUFORM are also used.

The market for CAD/CAM is vast, and a number of companies compete in this area. Computervision Corporation (a pioneer in the field), IBM, Prime, Gerber Scientific, Inc., Intergraph Corporation, and Hewlett-Packard are a few of the players after this billion-dollar market. IBM, for example, says it "donated $50 million in CAD/CAM systems or cash grants to twenty-two U.S. universities in 1983, to encourage manufacturing systems engineering education."

If the idea of using sophisticated computer systems to improve America's factories excites you, why not consider becoming involved in computer-aided design and computer-aided manufactur-

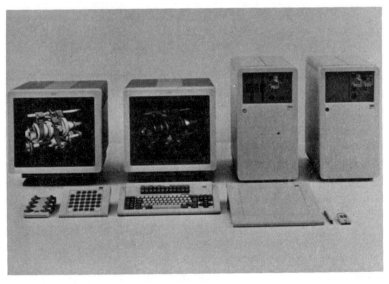

COURTESY IBM

The IBM 5080 graphic system.

ing. By so doing, you will help make our factories competitive with the rest of the world.

As mentioned at the beginning of this chapter, software specialists have yet another employment option: to work for an in-house data processing department of a large company, such as an oil company, a bank, or an insurance company. If you have the right résumé, you can pick the industry that interests you and go to work.

I asked Ruth K. Milburn of Esso Exploration, Inc., what software positions she could foresee in EXXON's future. She said that although systems software experts will continue to be in great demand, some applications programming jobs will disappear. She said that EXXON will continue to recruit college graduates with degrees in computer science, math, physics, and other relevant majors to fill openings for highly skilled technical programmers in the areas of petroleum exploration and reservoir engineering research. Furthermore, she noted that during the 1980's EXXON will pursue telecommunications and database specialists to staff its Telecommunications and Applications Support teams. Data security experts will also be in demand at EXXON, she said.

The opportunity to work with one of the world's most powerful computers may await you if you are hired by EXXON. Although EXXON uses IBM and Amdahl equipment, Ms. Milburn believes that the Cray will dominate exploration research in the years ahead.

A revealing question to ask yourself is whether you want to work for a large or small company. Since big corporations are able to fight for themselves, let me throw a carrot to the small software company. If you work for a dynamic small or medium-sized organization, you will not have a huge bureaucracy between you and top management. For this reason, you should have more personal input to the leadership of the company, and you might move into a management or an executive position sooner than if you work for a company with ten thousand employees.

And last of all, the U.S., state, and local governments are major employers of software talent, many of whom are from minority groups. Many government agencies, from the Defense Communications Agency to the Federal Bureau of Investigation and the National Security Agency, employ people who are trained to work with computers. The National Institutes of Health and the National Oceanic and Atmospheric Administration also might wish to hire you, especially if you are a computer scientist, a mathematician, or an electronics or software engineer.

A "fisheye" lens view of the flight deck of the Space Shuttle Orbiter 102 Columbia. Each crew member has a hand controller for controlling the spacecraft. The controller provides information to the computer system, which in turn records attitude changes. On the commander's side is a translation controller for moving the vehicle along any axis in flight. Between the two positions for the crew members are the flight computer and navigation aid console. Immediately in front of the console are the three CRTs used to display computer data and information for the crew. On either side of the CRT are such flight instruments as the altitude direction indicator and horizontal situation indicator, as well as air speed and direction finders.

If your qualifications match the job you seek, the U.S. Office of Personnel Management (OPM) will add your name to its list of eligibles. Some agencies such as the CIA bypass the OPM competitive service procedures and hire directly.

Jobs with the government are classified by Civil Service grade levels like GS-5 or GS-15. The higher the GS rating, the higher the salary and, in general, the more demanding the position.

Some of you may dream of working for the National Aeronautics and Space Administration. During an interview with Steve Nesbitt, Public Information Officer for the Lyndon B. Johnson Space Center, Houston, Nesbitt told me that the Center has approximately 3,400 Civil Service employees, of whom several hundred have programming responsibilities. They do every type of computer programming, from payroll to scheduling astronaut activities. Nesbitt said that NASA has a small but steady need for programmers to fill these positions.

Nesbitt explained that the majority of the work on the shuttle is awarded to support contractors. Some of the main ones are Lockheed Corporation, Computer Sciences Corporation, IBM, and Singer-Link.

Nesbitt also mentioned that NASA's computers analyze data from the Earth Resources Satellites. In polar orbit, they scan the earth every nine days gathering information on crops, forests, and soil conditions.

NASA has nine installations, each of which conducts its own recruiting. NASA's headquarters is in Washington, DC, where it "exercises management over the space flight centers, research centers, and other installations..."

NASA Langley Research Center in Hampton, VA, conducts "research and technology development in aeronautics and space and the application of technology to environment quality and monitoring."

NASA Goddard Space Flight Center, Greenbelt, MD, and Wallops Flight Facility, Wallops Island, VA, conduct "and are responsible for all the facets of remotely controlled earth orbiting and sounding rocket missions." The Center at Wallops Island "develops, maintains and operates a research airport in support of NASA's aeronautical research programs..."

NASA Ames Research Center, Moffett Field, CA, conducts "basic and applied research in physical and life science areas of vital importance to the advancement of aeronautics and space technology."

John F. Kennedy Space Center, NASA Kennedy Space Center, FL, is "NASA's major launch operations facility and is the primary site for launchings of the manned Space Shuttle vehicles and payloads."

NASA George C. Marshall Space Flight Center, Huntsville, AL, serves as "one of NASA's primary Centers for the design, development, integration and testing of space transportation systems and high energy stages for orbital transfer and deep space missions; design and development of payload carriers and the integration of science and applications payloads into carrier vehicles; and other systems for present and future space exploration."

NASA Lyndon B. Johnson Space Center, Houston, TX, manages the "development and operation of the Space Shuttle, a manned space transportation system being developed for the United States by NASA. The Shuttle is being designed to reduce the cost of using space for commercial, scientific, and defense needs."

NASA Lewis Research Center, Cleveland, OH, has a "critical role in conceiving and directing the nation's aerospace propulsion and power programs."

National Space Technology Laboratories, NSTL Station, MS, supports "testing of Space Shuttle Main Engine and Main Propulsion Test Article."

If you desire further information about positions with NASA, write the agency for its Career Opportunities pamphlets, which include Careers in Aerospace Mathematician, Electronics Engineer, and Systems Analyst.

Defense agencies and military research organizations need computer personnel. The Departments of the Army, Navy, and Air Force will recruit you (many jobs also are civilian) to solve their information systems and engineering problems. The Naval Research Laboratory hires computer-oriented graduates to do software engineering, systems analysis, and software systems specifications as well as work on artificial intelligence research. For a comprehensive list of opportunities available with federal agencies, look under "Employer Profiles/ U.S. Government" in *Peterson's Engineering, Science and Computer Jobs.*

All five branches of the service will train you in computers from the ground up; however, they will want to commit you to from two to six years of active service. The National Guard or reserves initially require only six months' active duty, but the competition for these assignments is stiff.

Nothing illustrates the breadth of the software industry better than a glance at the *ICP Software Directory*, published by International Computer Programs, Inc., 9000 Keystone Crossing, P.O. Box 40946, Indianapolis, IN 46240. This enormous resource includes over 20,000 software products from over 5,000 vendors and is divided into the following volumes:

Volume 1: Systems Software
Volume 2: General Accounting Systems
Volume 3: Management & Administrative Systems
Volume 4: Banking, Insurance and Finance Systems
Volume 5: Manufacturing & Engineering Systems
Volume 6: Specialized Industry Systems
Volume 7: Microcomputer Systems

The vendors listed are at least potential employers of qualified individuals, although many factors will determine whether any single company is looking for software talent when you are ready to go to work. Companies with extensive computer libraries should have part or all of this directory on hand.

What will the world be like when you are ready to enter the job market? Which players will have changed? What technological barriers will be pierced by the tremendous innovative force of America's intensely dedicated computer professionals? Only the hazy depths of the crystal ball know where the cutting edge will lead us.

Perhaps the best way to catch a glimpse of the future is to look at the direction in which we are headed by considering the long-range research goals of a portion of the high-tech community. Microelectronics and Computer Technology Corporation says that its "programs and basic challenge for each include:

Software technology: Increase the productivity and reduce the cost of software development, testing, and verification through improved methods, tools, and architectures.

VLSI/CAD: Significantly reduce design costs and improve engineering productivity related to the layout of Very Large Scale Integrated circuits (VLSI) through development of improved computer-aided design (CAD) systems.

Semiconductor packaging: Develop methods of making connections to and interconnecting semiconductor chips to take advantage of anticipated advances in complex semiconductor chips.

Parallel processing: Develop the languages and architectures to allow computers to perform tasks simultaneously instead of sequentially, with corresponding increases in processing speed.

Database system management: Improve database design, storage methods, and capacities to permit flexible storage and faster retrieval of a broader range of more complex information.

Human factors technology: Improve the relationship between man and computer by simplifying the use of computers through techniques such as improved voice or character recognition or use of natural languages.

Artificial intelligence knowledge based systems: Realize the computer's problem-solving potential by developing new ways to

COURTESY NASA

Man and computer—a partnership for creativity.

represent human knowledge and thought concepts, as well as new engineering models and tools to apply human expertise to a wide range of problems."

I will venture that America will leap right over these so-called technological barriers and that some of you will provide the software power to help clear the fences. To quote the president of Digital Equipment Corporation, Kenneth H. Olsen: "Computers are making work more interesting, making it more fun, making it more satisfying. That's the business we're in—we're having more fun at it than ever before, and there is no end in sight."

Glossary

A

ADA   Computer programming language commissioned by the Department of Defense.

algorithm   Sequence of formulas or logical steps.

applications program   Computer program that solves problems for the end-user, e.g., a payroll program.

applications programmer   Person who writes (codes) the instructions that enable a computer to solve a specific problem.

applications software   Set of programs that solve problems for the end-user.

*artificial intelligence   Subfield of computer science that is concerned with symbolic reasoning and problem-solving.

assembler computer program that translates an assembler language into numeric machine language.

assembler language   Hardware-dependent computer language that allows a programmer to write instructions to the computer using alphabetic symbols rather than binary machine language. Usually one machine language instruction is generated per statement.

asynchronous   Transmitting binary characters at random time intervals. The speed of the transmission of characters is controlled by the sending device rather than by the communication medium, which is usually a modem and a telephone line.

B

BASIC language   *B*eginner's *A*ll-purpose *S*ymbolic *I*nstruction *C*ode. Developed at Dartmouth College, BASIC is a popular programming language among microcomputer users; it is generally easier to learn than other languages.

batch processing   Collecting and processing input data in a single run rather than on-line.

binary   Numbering system based on 2 rather than 10. The two digits used are zero (0) and (1), which can correspond to "off" or "on" (low voltage/high voltage). Electronic digital computers are binary in nature.

bug In software: a defect in a computer program caused by an error or omission. In hardware: a defect in the circuitry. The term was coined when a moth short-circuited one of the earliest electronic computers.

C

card reader Machine that "reads" holes that have been punched in an IBM card in a special code called the Hollerith code.

cathode ray rube (CRT) Computer video display screen.

central processing unit (CPU) The internal main "brain" of a computer, generally consisting of the arithmetic and logic unit, the control unit, and sometimes main storage.

chip Tiny silicon wafer with computer circuits etched on it; sometimes called an integrated circuit.

CICS Customer Information Control System; the IBM teleprocessing monitor.

cipher Message that has been translated into an incomprehensible code.

COBOL *CO*mmon *B*usiness *O*riented *L*anguage, high-level programming language written in English-like statements; widely used for business applications programming.

compatibility Quality that enables a program to be executed on different models of computer hardware.

compiler Programming language translator that is capable of generating instructions that a computer can understand from symbolic coding. A COBOL compiler, for example, can create more than one machine instruction from one English-like instruction.

computer-aided design (CAD) Computer system that enables engineers and others to design products with the aid of a sophisticated graphics terminal.

computer-aided manufacturing (CAM) Automation of factories by placing the manufacturing process under the control of a sophisticated computer system.

computer-integrated manufacturing (CIM) Complex computer system that combines computer-aided design (CAD) and computer-aided manufacturing (CAM).

computerese Computer jargon.

configuration of computer system The way computer equipment is grouped together to form an interconnected system. A typical mainframe computer system might consist of a CPU, ten disk drives, four tape drives, two printers, a teleprocessing control unit, and other machines all connected by cables.

cursor   Blinking rectangle or bright mark on a computer display screen that indicates where a character can be entered.

D

database management system (DBMS)   Electronic file control program that facilitates "instant" access and update to information located on secondary storage, usually computer disks.

database   Huge electronic file usually stored on a disk(s). Information can be accessed instantly from a computer terminal or personal computer.

data communications (DC)   Transmission of data from one computer or terminal to another via telephone line, microwave, satellite, or other method.

data communications network   System of computers or terminals connected to a central computer or to each other. Terminals on the network can "talk" with the central computer or even to each other.

data communications software   Complex programs that make possible the transfer of information from one computer to another or from one terminal to another.

data communications specialist   Expert in the transmission of data using sophisticated communications software and specialized hardware such as modems and multiplexers.

data communications system   Network control software, computer hardware, and communication medium such as telephone lines, satellite transmission, fiber optics, and the like.

data processing (DP)   Collective term generally referring to the use of computers and computer equipment to solve information problems.

decrypt   To decode (translate) a coded message back into readable form.

disk (hard)   Fast mass storage device allowing direct access of data.

disk drive   Device for "reading" and "writing" data on disks.

diskette (floppy)   Small, thin plastic disk coated with iron oxide that spins inside a Teflon-lined envelope, used for secondary storage of data, especially on microcomputers.

distributed data processing   General term for a way of computing in which small computer systems are placed at geographically separate locations but connected by telephone lines.

distributed database   Information stored on electronic files, usually disks, at several remote points.

documentation   Explanatory information about a computer program or a set of related computer programs.

documentor   Person who assembles and writes explanatory information about a computer program or set of related programs.

DOS   Disk operating system, group of supervisory systems programs contained on a disk.

download   To accept data from the central computer.

E

electronic mail   Computer system whereby persons can transfer information (like memos and letters) back and forth. Most systems use passwords to insure privacy.

encrypt   To encode (translate) a message into an unreadable code.

expert system   Computer system that has the knowledge of human experts incorporated into the program.

external device   Hardware that is not an internal part of the computer, such as a tape drive.

F

fiber optics transmission system   System by which transparent fibers that "conduct" light are used to transmit modulated light. The signals can be decoded into characters in the transmission of information.

flowchart   Chart using special symbols that shows the sequence of a combination of operations that a programmer wants the computer to perform. Used to illustrate graphically the logic of a program.

FORTRAN language   *FOR*mula *TRAN*slator, high-level programming language that uses algebraic expressions and arithmetic statements; popular among mathematicians, scientists, and engineers.

H

hardware   The physical computer equipment, but not the programs.

high-level language   Programming language such as COBOL with a compiler that can generate many machine instructions per instruction written by the programmer.

I

independent contract programmer   Free-lance programmer.

independent software organization (ISO)   Type of company that specializes in producing computer programs but does not manufacture hardware.

integrate   To combine the capabilities of several types of programs into one system, using one set of commands. Integrated software might have, for example, the ability to handle the following variety of tasks: word processing, spreadsheet functions, database management, and business graphics in a single application package. Integration of many functions also might be achieved through the operating system.

integrated circuit (IC)   Tiny circuit imprinted on a single semiconductor chip.

interface   Common boundary or interconnection between parts of a computer system or two computer systems.

J

job control language (JCL)   Series of statements that direct a computer program that prepares each job for execution by the computer.

K

K   Kilobyte(s).

keypunch machine   Device that punches holes into cards arranged in a code that a computer can read.

keypunch operator   Person trained to operate a keypunch machine.

kilobyte   Approximately one thousand bytes; exactly 1,024 bytes.

*knowledge base   Base of information encoded in a knowledge representation for a particular application.

knowledge engineer   Highly educated professional who interviews experts and attempts to incorporate their knowledge into a computer system.

*knowledge engineering   Engineering discipline whereby knowledge is integrated into computer systems in order to solve complex problems normally requiring a high level of human expertise.

*knowledge representation   Formal term for representing facts and rules about a subject or specialty.

*knowledge systems   Computer systems that embody knowledge, including inexact, heuristic, and subjective knowledge; the results of knowledge engineering.

L

low-level language   Assembler languages; so called because an assembler (translator program) usually generates one binary machine instruction for each symbolic instruction written by the programmer.

M

machine   Trade term for computer.

machine code   Binary code that a computer understands.

mainframe computer   Large computer system as opposed to mini- or microcomputer.

maintenance (hardware)   Repair of computer equipment.

maintenance (software)   Improvements, changes, and corrections made to computer programs.

management information consultant   Adviser to clients in information handling.

microcomputer   Small-scale, relatively inexpensive computer built around a microprocessor.

microprocessor   Main "brain" or CPU of a microcomputer that is built on a single chip.

minicomputer   Computer that is physically smaller than a mainframe. Minicomputers are generally more powerful than microcomputers.

modem   *MO*dulator *DEM*odulator, device that converts the bits (binary digits) from a computer into analog signals (a range of frequencies). The modem then sends the converted data over a telephone line, at the other end of which the reverse occurs.

N

network   See *data communications network.*

O

object code   Binary machine language resulting from the translation by a compiler or assembler that a specific computer can understand.

operating system (OS)   The systems software that controls the internal operations of the computer as well as the input and output.

on-line   Way to access the central computer using video display terminals or personal computers. Data can be entered as it occurs.

P

peripheral equipment   Auxiliary machines such as magnetic tape drives, printers, and terminals that are partially under the control of the computer.

personal computer   Small computer built around a microprocessor.

portable programs   Programs that can run on different types of computers with minimum changes.

program   Series of instructions that tell a computer what to do.

programmer Person who writes or codes the instructions that tell a computer what to do.

programmer/analyst Computer professional who designs and writes computer programs.

program maintenance Changes, additions, and improvements to a previously written program.

protocols Conventions that govern the flow of data between terminals and computers.

R

record Group of related fields that are treated as a unit, such as a name and address record.

S

security software Access control and encryption programs used to protect computer files.

semiconductor Material used in computer memories, such as silicon, whose conductivity is between that of an insulator and that of a metal.

service bureau Company that sells turnkey software services. It develops software to solve general or specialized business problems, runs the programs on its own or a rented computer, and delivers the output to the customer.

software General term for computer programs.

software engineer Person capable of designing, coding, and testing sophisticated software such as CAD/CAM systems.

spreadsheet Applications program with powerful recalculation features that refigure all numbers affected by a change to any related number. One use of a spreadsheet is to set up budget projections.

support As applied to computers, the advice and help offered by software or hardware producers.

supercomputer Superscale processors used for scientific "number-crunching." Supercomputers have massive memories and are capable of the fastest processing speeds.

supermicrocomputer Powerful microcomputer built around a 32-bit chip (with a 16-bit bus). This means that the CPU can process internally 32 bits at one time.

superminicomputer Powerful minicomputer built around a 32-bit-per-word processor.

synchronous Determining the speed of transmission of data by the communication medium, usually a modem and a telephone line.

systems analyst Programmer or other professional capable of designing computer programs.

systems integrator   Company that specializes in buying computers, display terminals, printers, and other equipment and bundling these components together with systems and proprietary applications software to create a complete computer system.

systems network architecture (SNA)   IBM's master plan for data communications.

systems programmer   Computer programmer capable of implementing complex systems software.

systems software   Programs that supervise the inner workings of the computer.

systems software designer   Computer professional who designs the complex systems software that supervises and supports the inner workings of the computer.

tape (magnetic)   Secondary information storage medium where data is held sequentially in the form of magnetically polarized spots on a reel of tape coated with iron oxide.

tape drive   Device for "reading" and "writing" data on a magnetic tape.

teleprocessing (TP)   Transmission of data from one computer or terminal to another, usually over a telephone system.

terminal   Input-output device such as a CRT with attached keyboard that enables the user to input data into a computer or receive data from a computer.

test-condition   Set of circumstances evaluated to determine action.

U

upload   To move data from an "intelligent" terminal or personal computer to the massive files on a mainframe.

user-friendly   Computer software and hardware that is easy to use.

W

word processor   Applications program that allows the user to make changes and correct errors on the screen before printing on paper.

---

*Definitions courtesy of Teknowledge, Inc. of Palo Alto, California.